SEW MUCH LOVE

Sweet & Stylish Sewing and Quilting Projects to Cherish

16 BEAUTIFUL PROJECTS TO SEW

Lesley Domier

TUVA

Tuva Publishing

www.tuvapublishing.com

Address Merkez Mah. Cavusbasi Cad. No: 71
Cekmekoy - Istanbul 34782 / Türkiye
Tel: +9 0216 642 62 62

Sew Much Love

First Print 2025 / May

All Global Copyrights Belong to
Tuva Tekstil ve Yayıncılık Ltd.

Content Sewing / Patchwork

Editor in Chief Ayhan DEMİRPEHLİVAN

Project Editor Kader DEMİRPEHLİVAN

Designer Lesley DOMIER

Technical Editor Leyla ARAS

Graphic Designers Ömer ALP, Abdullah BAYRAKÇI,
Tarık TOKGÖZ, Yunus GÜLDOĞAN

Photograph Tuva Publishing

ISBN 978-605-7834-87-4

The EEA authorised representative is Authorised Rep Compliance
Ltd. Ground Floor, 71 Lower Baggot Street, Dublin, DO2 P593, Ireland
(www.arccompliance.com)

TuvaPublishing

CONTENTS

INTRODUCTION 5

PROJECT GALLERY 6

TECHNIQUES 8

PROJECTS

INTRODUCTION

Welcome to my imagination! It is a colourful space where my love of miniature prints is woven into the fabric of all I design. The teeny-tiny of quilting has met its match, and I am here to show you, step- by-step, how to incorporate my passion and innovative techniques into your carefully curated projects. I share tricks and sneaky little steps to simplify the process, and help you fashion a lifestyle that invites a relaxing and organized creative space.

I share how to paper-piece a hexie pincushion, my secret steps to construct a Dresden block like you have never seen before, how to use 1 inch squares for the Sew Much Love pillow, and all the brilliant ways to make and use fabric stamps.

Setting aside time to hand make gifts is precious, and my desire is to share what I have learned to help you streamline your time. These projects range from a few hours to a day-and walk away from your sewing machine with a warm heart and deeply satisfied with your work. My hope is that you will feel rewarded by your passion, and continue to build a fruitful addiction to which many around you will reap the benefits of!

Lesley

PROJECT GALLERY

P.20

P.26

P.30

P.34

P.40

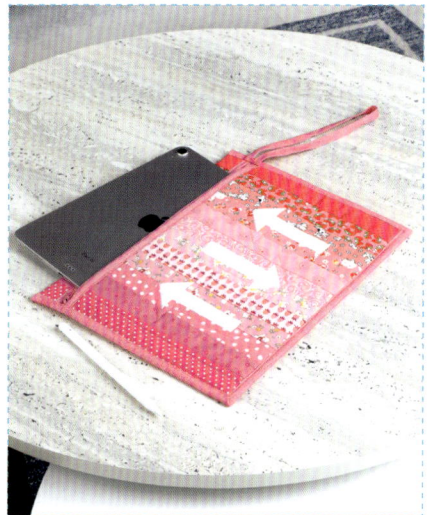

P.44

P.50

P.56

P.62

P.68

P.72

P.80

P.84

P.90

P.96

P.102

BASIC PAPER PIECING INSTRUCTIONS

STEP 1: Fold the template on the stitching line between pieces a and b (Figure 1). Unfold the template.

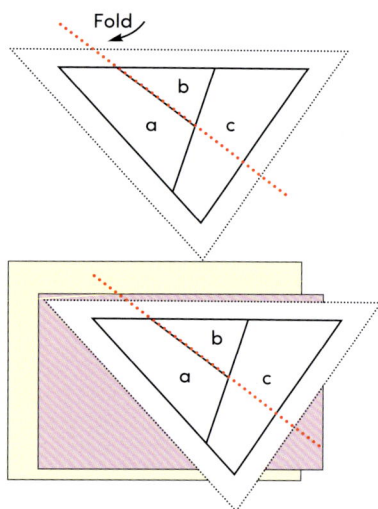

Figure 1

STEP 2: Using a piece of fabric large enough to cover piece a and the seam allowance around it, place the reverse side of the fabric to the back of the foundation template. Using a piece of fabric large enough to cover piece b, place it right sides together with fabric covering piece a (Figure 2).

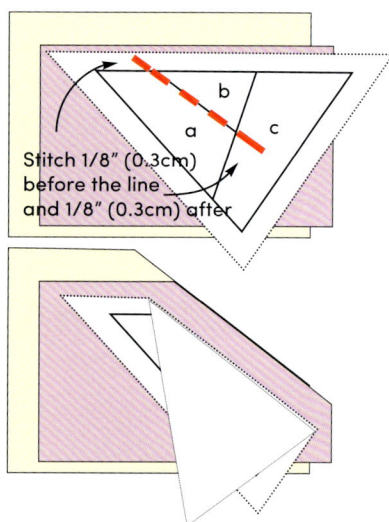

Figure 2

To ensure that your piece b fabric is in the correct position, align it while the template is folded. At the least, it should cover the area when folded.

STEP 3: Carefully pick up the fabric and template set and move to your machine. Unfold the template and stitch the line between a and b. Start sewing ⅛" (0.3cm) before the line and stitch ⅛" (0.3cm) beyond the line.

STEP 4: With the template folded on the line, trim the seam allowance ⅛" (0.3cm) to ⅜" (1cm) from the folded edge of the template.

STEP 5: Fold fabric the seam and finger press.

STEP 6: Repeat steps 1 through 6 for each numbered piece working sequentially (e.g. a/b, b/c, c/d).

STEP 7: Gently tear away foundation from the extra stitching in piece c to the line between pieces b and c.

STEP 8: Repeat steps 1 through 7 for each letered piece working sequentially (e.g. a/b, b/c, c/d).

STEP 9: Once the piece is completed, trim to the seam allowance.

Repeat for each template.

Joining the Template Pieces

Using your desired pattern, sew all of your template pieces using the Basic Paper Piecing Instructions.

With right sides together, place a straight pin through the points on the corners on both ends. Use pins or fabric clips along the seam as necessary. If the seam alignment is critical, baste those areas to ensure that your seams align before your final stitching. After joining two template pieces, ensure that they are properly aligned.

Remove the paper from the seam allowance only before adding the next template piece. Complete each block or panel for your pattern.

Join the blocks or panels using the pattern as a guide. Use pins or fabric clips to match critical seam alignments. If your foundation paper is making it difficult to match seams for these panels, remove the paper backing being careful to not stretch the fabric. Otherwise, remove the paper backing after all piecing has been completed.

General Paper Piecing Tips

Align a piece of cardstock on the line you intend to fold. Fold to the cardstock. Remove the cardstock and crease your fold.

Always overestimate the size of fabric you'll need for each piece PLUS the seam allowances. Select a thread that blends with most of your fabrics. Use an open-front presser foot which allows you to clearly see your stitching. Set your stitch length to 14 to 18 stitches per inch. Mistakes happen! Keep a seam ripper handy.

Tiny Tips

If you're having difficulty catching the fabric on the feed dogs as you slide it in place to stitch, slip a scrap of paper under the unit being sewn before sliding it under the needle. Tear away the scrap paper after stitching.

Trim thread tails after each seam.

Finger pressing will be sufficient for these tiny pieces, but if you do need to press, use a hot, dry iron.

After joining pieces and panels, trim seam allowances that extend beyond the pattern template. Have tweezers handy to remove small pieces of paper.

MAKING BINDING STRIPS

Straight Cut Binding:

1 Cut strip from selvedge to selvedge. I prefer 2 ¼"
(5.5cm) wide strips for smaller projects and 2 ½"
(6cm) wide strips for quilts.

2 Cut enough strips to make a continuous binding
to cover the perimeter of your project and add an
extra 10" (25.5cm) to the length.

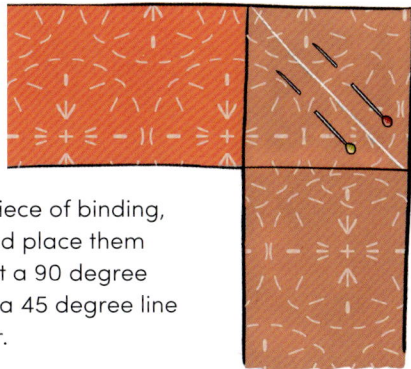

3 To make a long piece of binding,
take two strips and place them
right sides together at a 90 degree
angle and pin. Draw a 45 degree line
from corner to corner.

4 Stitch across the corner on the drawn
line.

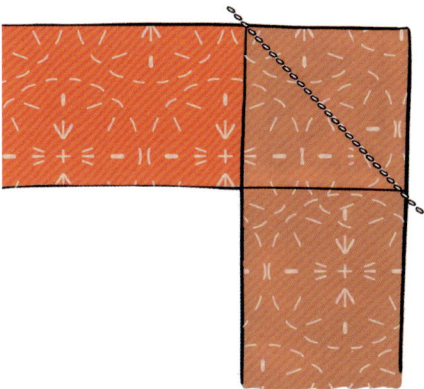

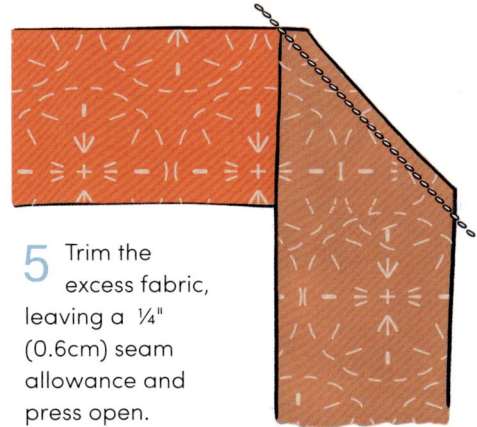

5 Trim the
excess fabric,
leaving a ¼"
(0.6cm) seam
allowance and
press open.

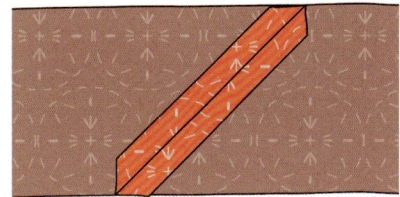

6 Continue sewing strips together until you have
enough to cover the perimeter of your project.
strips together until you have enough to cover the
perimeter of your project.

7 Fold the binding in half lengthwise, wrong sides
together, and press.

Bias Cut Binding:

1 Cut strips at a 45 degree angle to the selvedge. Cut 1 ½" (3.8cm) wide strips for
single fold binding and 2 ¼" (5.5cm) wide or 2 ½" (6cm) wide strips for double
fold binding.

2 Follow Step 2 –Step 6 for straight cut binding.

3 Fold the binding in half lengthwise, wrong sides together, and press. You can
skip this step for single fold binding.

BINDING A PROJECT

1 Start by placing the binding on the right side of the quilt, aligning the raw edges. Make sure to leave a tail and start 5" – 10" (13 – 25.5cm) away from the corner of one side.

2 Use a walking foot and a ¼" (0.6cm) wide seam allowance to stitch the binding strip to the quilt. Stop ¼" (0.6cm) from the first corner and stitch up to the corner at a 45 degree angle.

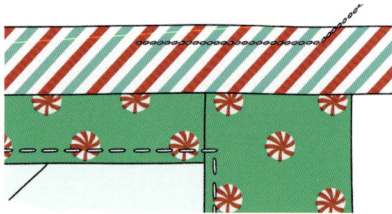

3 Pull the quilt out of the machine and fold the binding up and away from the quilt so that the fold forms a 45 degree angle.

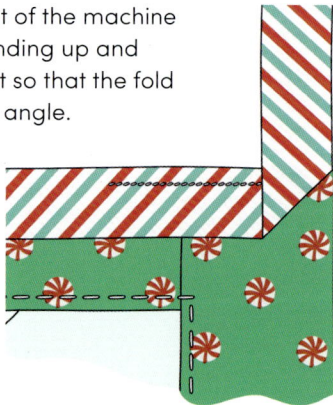

4 Then fold the binding back down onto itself making sure to align the raw edges with the quilt. Continue stitching the binding strip to the quilt and repeat all the way around.

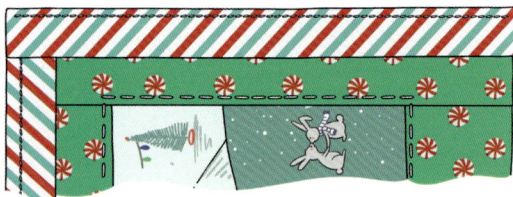

5 When you are about 5" – 10" (13 – 25.5cm) away from the starting point, pull the quilt out of the machine and trim the tails of binding so they overlap by the exact width of the binding. (ie. if your binding is 2 ¼" (5.5cm) wide, the tails should overlap by 2 ¼" (5.5cm), if your binding is 2 ½" (6cm) wide, they should overlap by 2 ½" (6cm))

An easy way to get the exact width of the binding is by cutting a little piece of binding off.

Next, open up the little binding cut off and place it on top of the overlapping binding tails. Match up the end with the bottom binding tail.

Cut off the excess on the top binding tail.

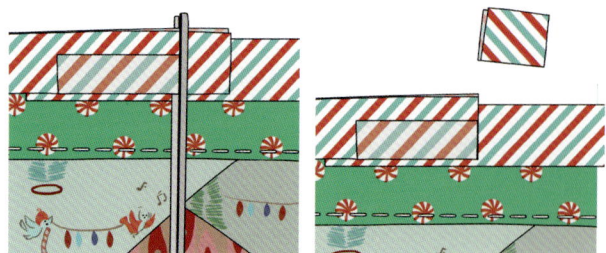

6 Place the binding ends right sides together, at right angles and pin together.

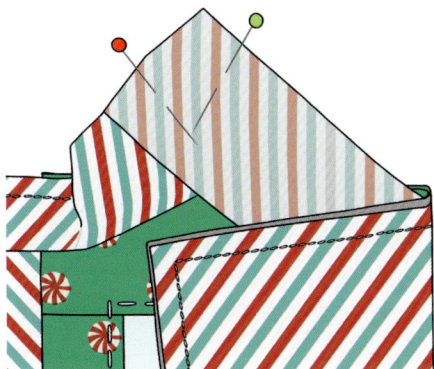

7 Draw a diagonal line and sew together. Trim the seam allowance to a ¼" (0.6cm). Press the seam open and fold the binding back in half. Continue sewing the binding to the quilt.

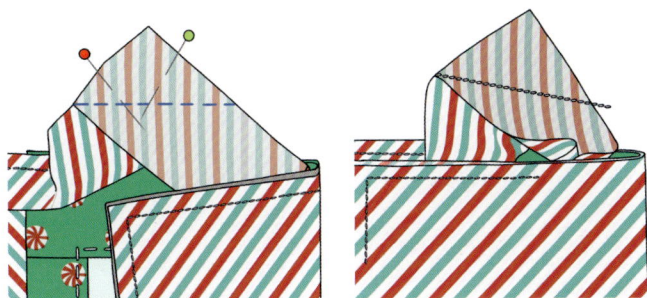

8 Wrap the binding to the back of the quilt. Pin and stitch the binding to the quilt back as desired.

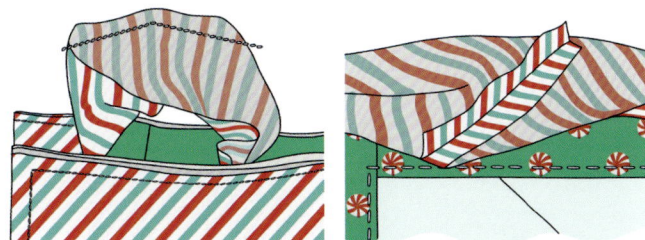

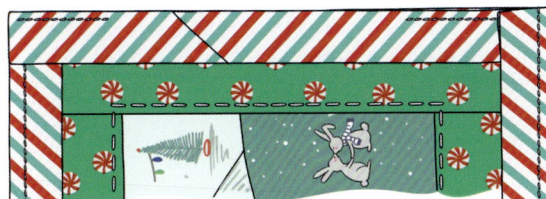

QUILTING

1 Mark quilting lines on the right side of your quilt top. I like to use a Hera marker or a water and air soluble pen.

2 Make a quilt sandwich by layering the backing right side down, batting, and then the quilt top right side up. Baste as desired. I like to pin baste or thread baste smaller projects and spray glue baste quilt tops.

3 Quilt and bind as desired.

HAND QUILTING

1 Thread your needle with one strand of quilting thread or pearl cotton.

2 Make a knot at the end of the thread.

3 Insert your needle through the right side of your quilt top a bit away from where you'd like to make your first stitch. Draw the needle out on the right side at the starting point and pull the thread taut to draw the knot through the quilt top so it is hidden in the batting.

4 Make a backstitch and then quilt with a running stitch.

HAND STITCHES

Running Stitch

Knot the end of your thread and bring your needle up at 1, down at 2, up at three and down at four. With this stitch, you need to try and keep your stitches at regular intervals and keep even tension to avoid your stitches from puckering. Use a Hera marker or disappearing pen to mark your lines.

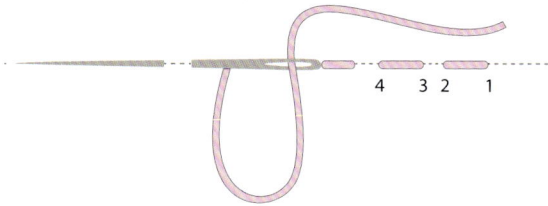

Blind Stitch

The most commonly used stitch for appliquéing onto a background.

Knot the end of a single thread and bring your needle up through the back of your background fabric barely piercing the edge of the piece you are appliquéing. Place the needle back into the background fabric right next to where you came out and bring the needle back up through all the fabrics about 1/16" (0.2cm) from the last stitch. Continue all the way around your appliqué piece. Take the needle and thread to the back of your work and knot to finish.

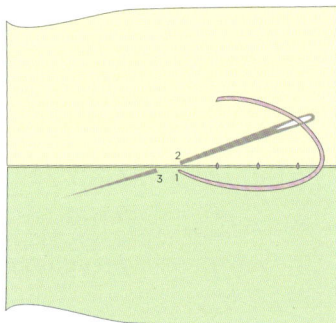

FINISHING STITCHES

Top Stitch: 1/4" (0.6cm) away from the seam

Edge Stitch: 1/8" (0.3cm) away from the seam

Under Stitch: Press the seam allowance towards the lining and stitch 1/8" (0.3cm) to 1/4" (0.6cm) away from the seam line on the lining. Press the lining toward the inside of the item. The lining will lay flat with a crisp edge, preventing it from rolling out of place.

Back Stitch

When working this stitch try to keep your stitches at an even, consistent length for a smooth line. Bring your thread up from behind your work at point 1 and take it backwards and down through your fabric at point 2. Then bring it back up, one stitch length in front (this will be point 3) and then down again at point 1. Continue this pattern, remembering to keep your stitches at a consistent length.

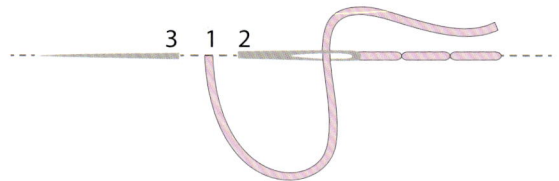

Whip Stitch

Knot one end of your single thread. Push your needle and thread through both layers of fabric only catching a few threads from both. Take the needle to the back and bring it back through both layers again.

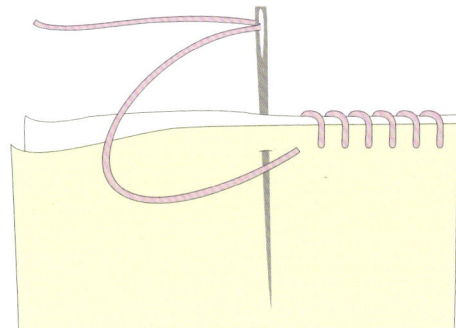

Ladder Stitch

An invisible stitch used to sew two folded edges together. Moving from right to left, take a small stitch out of one side of the folded edge, then move forward and take a small stitch out of the other side. Every so often, pull the thread taut, so that the fabric edges close and the stitches vanish.

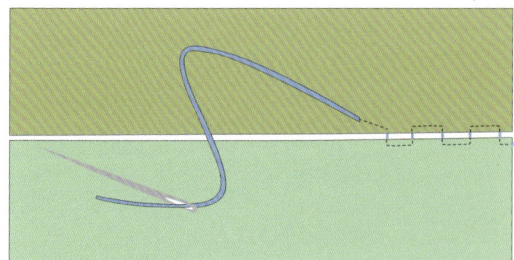

TEMPLATES

I love templates. If and when I can, I'll always make a template of whatever it is I am making because they save me so much time and effort. Especially if I'm planning on making more than one of a project. Instead of having to always measure the exact amount, all I have to do is place my template on my fabric or interfacing and trace. Doesn't fit? Move on to a bigger piece of fabric. This probably comes from my years of garment design and sewing, where drawing out a pattern piece just from measurements will not work. If you haven't used templates before, I'd definitely recommend giving it a try because it is such a time saver!

Templates can be made from cardstock, manila paper, and yup, even your cereal box for smaller projects! I have a roll of manila that I use for garment patterns and letter sized cardstock that I use for smaller projects. Another option I've been adding more of to my own stash of templates are from the clear plastic you can buy by the sheet or as a packaged bundle. Clear plastic templates make fussy cutting super easy and I can always make sure all the prints are aligned and where I want them to be.

Experiment, see which type of template you prefer, and don't forget to label them for future use!

How to Organize Templates

Pattern hooks are an excellent way of organizing your templates, but zip lock bags work wonderful too! My bigger patterns get hung on a pattern hook and smaller projects get their designated zip lock bag keeping all the little templates safely together until I'm ready to work on them again. You don't need anything fancy, just something to keep your templates together and labeled for easy access.

Making Templates

Photocopy or trace the templates in the book. You can use copy paper templates but a heavier cardstock or clear template plastic is recommended.

Tracing the Templates

Templates with seam allowance included:
Place your fabric right side up. Trace around the template and cut out on the traced line.

Templates without seam allowance included:
Place your fabric right side down. Trace around the template. Use a ruler to draw a ¼" (0.6cm) seam allowance around the piece and cut out along the seam allowance line.

PATCHWORK

Hand Piecing

1 Thread a needle with one strand of thread and tie a knot at the end of the thread.

2 Place two pieces of fabric right sides together and pin.

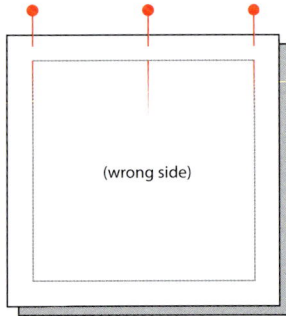

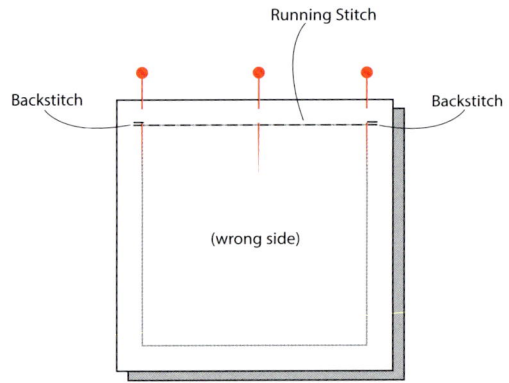

(wrong side)

Running Stitch

Backstitch   Backstitch

(wrong side)

3 Starting from right to left, insert your needle at your tracing line and make one backstitch in the seam allowance.

4 Sew a running stitch to the the opposite tracing line and smooth out any wrinkles made while sewing.

5 Make one backstitch in the seam allowance and then knot.

6 Press the seam allowance toward the darker fabric.

(wrong side)

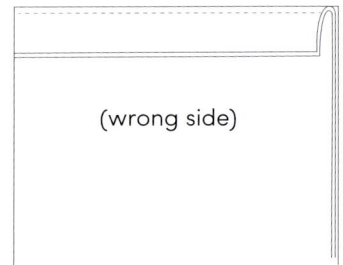

Machine Piecing

1 Place two pieces of fabric right sides together and pin.

2 Stitch together using a ¼" (0.6cm) seam allowance.

3 To stitch two sets together, nest the center seams and stitch in place.

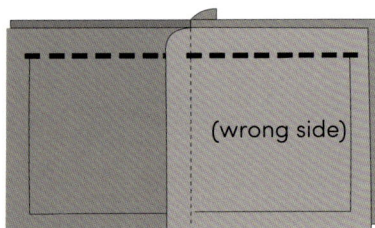

(wrong side)

4 Press the seam allowance to one side.

Piecing Patchwork with Inset Seams

If you're like me, you like to switch off between EPP (English Paper Piecing), FPP (Foundation Paper Piecing) and hand piecing. When you EPP you don't have to think about inset seams and most of the time that goes for FPP as well. With hand piecing however, that's something to keep in mind when piecing certain shapes such as hexagons and diamonds.

1 Stitch the first two pieces together, starting and stopping at the seam allowance. Make sure to backstitch where you start and stop but avoid stitching in the seam allowance.

2 Attach the next piece using the same process as in step 1.

3 Sew along the remaining side using the same process as in step 1.

4 Press the seam allowance open.

BASIC EPP - ENGLISH PAPER PIECING

English Paper Piecing is a patchwork technique where you wrap fabric around a paper template and then hand sew them together. You can thread baste or glue baste the fabric to the paper template, and I usually glue baste.

Most of the paper templates I use are small so I cut my fabric pieces with a ¼" (0.6cm) seam allowance. If you're working with bigger sized paper templates, cutting your fabric with a ⅜" (1cm) seam allowance is helpful.

When glue basting, make sure to not apply too much glue as that will make it hard to remove the templates later. Apply the glue in a thin line away from the edge of the paper template.

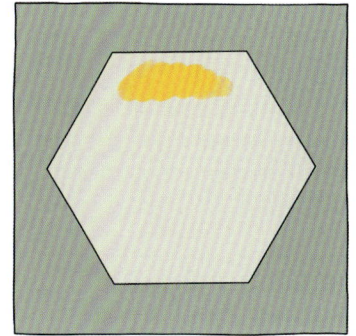

1 Place your fabric right side down and next center your paper template on top.

2 Apply a thin line of glue.

3 Fold over the fabric and press down.

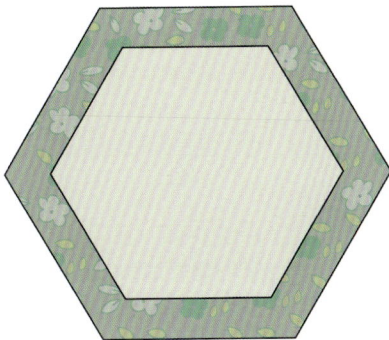

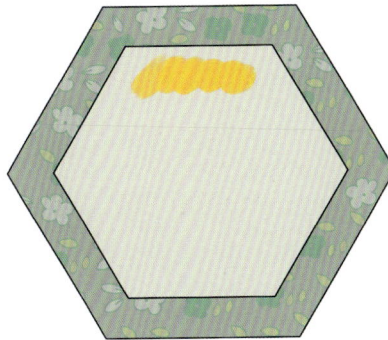

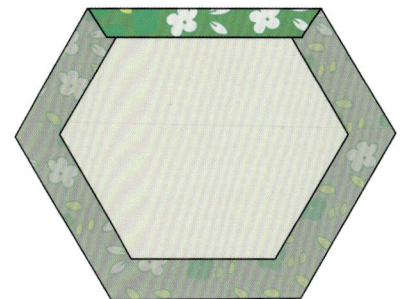

4 Repeat around the whole paper template until all sides are basted.

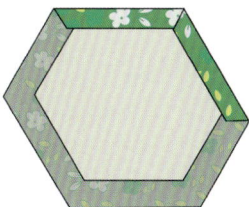

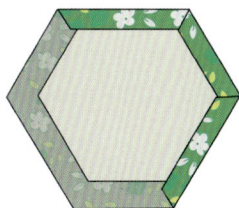

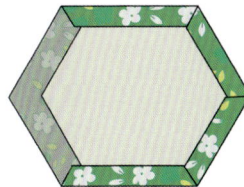

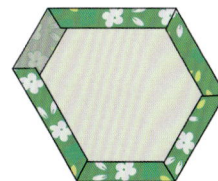

5 Once all your pieces are basted, stitch your shapes together using a whip stitch. Make sure to avoid stitching through the paper template and use small stitches. I prefer to use a 60wt thread in a neutral color with a size 11 milliners needle for piecing my EPP shapes together.

6 After stitching your shapes together, press to set the seam allowance and remove the paper templates.

7 Once all the paper templates are out, press again to flatten your patchwork panel.

APPLIQUÉ

There are a few methods to prepare your patchwork pieces for appliqué, and these are three of my favorite methods.

Raw Edge Appliqué Pieces with Fusible Web

1 Cut a piece of fabric that is a little bit bigger than your template and a matching size piece of fusible web. Fusible web has one glue side and one side backed with paper.

2 Fuse the web to the wrong side of the fabric.

3 Place the template on the paper backing and trace. Here you need to pay attention to the orientation of the template since you are tracing a mirror image. If it is a shape such as a circle or square, you don't need to worry about about which direction the template is facing.

4 Cut out your shape along the traced outline and peel off the paper.

5 Place on top of your backing fabric and fuse in place with a hot iron.

6 Decrease the stitch length on your sewing machine and stitch around the edge of the shape to secure it to the backing.

Appliqué Pieces with Light-Weight Sew-In Interfacing

1 Cut a piece of fabric that is a little bigger than your template and a matching piece of light-weight sew-in interfacing. Make sure to cut these two pieces big enough to trim around your template once traced.

2 Place the template on the interfacing and trace.

3 Place the interfacing on the RIGHT side of the fabric and stitch along the traced line. Make sure to backstitch when you start and stop to secure.

4 Cut out the shape, leaving an approximate ⅛"- ¼" (0.3-0.6cm) seam allowance past your stitching line.

5 Pull the interfacing apart from the fabric and cut a slit to turn right side out through.

6 Turn right side out through the slit and push out the edges of the fabric with a blunt object such as a chop stick or a Clover turning tool.

7 Once you've got the shape how you want it, press it flat on the fabric side.

8 Place on top of your backing fabric and pin or glue in place with a little bit of appliqué glue.

9 Stitch in place with a blind stitch or by machine.

Appliqué Pieces Shaped with Fusible Bating

A quick method for making perfect circles and other smooth round shapes using fusible bating.
Please see "Dresden Flower" using my cardstock technique for step by step instructions.

MATERIALS

* Pellon Lightweight Sew-in Interfacing (PLS36)
* Pellon 987f Fusible Fleece
* Pellon Shape-Flex Woven Interfacing SF101
* Pellon Extra Firm Fusible Interfacing Decor Bond
* Pellon Fusible Web
* Vinyl 16 gauge
* Warm and White Batting

* Warm and Natural Batting
* DMC Perle Cotton no. 5, no.8 and no.12 embroidery thread
* Gutermann Quilting Thread
* Superior Threads 60wt
* Aurifil 50wt
* Tsu Mu Gi 40wt

TOOLS

* Clover Hera Marker
* Clover Point Turner
* Clover Awl
* Seam Roller
* Glue Stick
* Glue Pen

* Appliqué Glue
* Ruler
* Rotary Cutter
* Scissors
* Needles
* Hemostat for Turning

* Seam Ripper
* Pins
* Bodkin
* Disappearing Pen/Marker
* Spray Glue for Basting
* Best Press for Starching

PROJECTS

MEADOW TABLE RUNNER

This lovely tablerunner reflects springtime meadows and deep green pastures. Scoop up your green toned fabrics and gorgeous little scraps to create this version all your own!

Finished Measurements
19 ¾" x 43 ¾" (50 x 111cm)

Materials Needed

✴ 8 - 10" (25.5cm) Square fabrics in various green shades

✴ 8 Yards (7.3m) of white or low volume fabric for the background

✴ 2 Yards (1.8m) for binding

✴ Matching sewing thread

✴ 22" x 45" (56 x 114cm) batting

From each 10" (25.5cm) square cut;

4 – 3" (8cm) squares

4 – 1 ¾" (4.5cm) squares

1 – 3 ½" (9cm) square

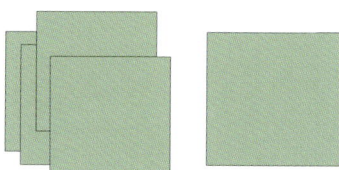

From the white or low volume print cut;

16 – 3" x 5 ½" (8 x 14cm) rectangles

16 – 1 ¾" x 3" (4.5 x 8cm) rectangles

24 – 1 ¾" (4.5cm) squares

8 – 4 ¼" (10.5cm) squares

5 – 3 ½" (9cm) squares – cut into half triangles

2 – 8 ½" (22cm) squares – cut into half triangles

3 – 1 ¾" x 42" (4.5 x 107cm) strips

Prepare the green squares for sewing by using a pen and ruler and draw a diagonal line from corner to corner.

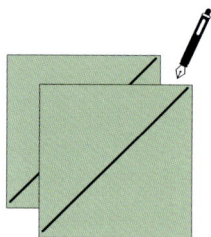

SEWING

1 Place a 1 ¾" (4.5cm) square with a white 1 ¾" x 3" (4.5 x 8cm) rectangle right sides facing lining up the square to one side.

2 Sew along the drawn line. Trim the excess fabric to ¼" (0.6cm). Fold the seam to the green fabric and place the next 1 ¾" (4.5cm) square on the opposite side. Sew it along the drawn line.

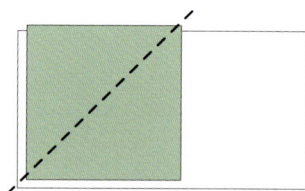

3 Trim the excess fabric to ¼" (0.6cm).

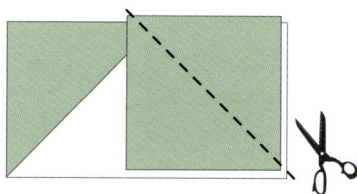

4 Press as shown by the arrows by pushing the iron towards the centre point and then on either side at the at the middle of the triangles first. This will help the

piece from distorting.

For the next steps you will need 3 of the white 1 ¾" (4.5cm) squares.

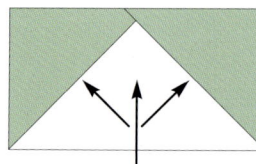

5 Sew one square to the right side of the previously sewn flying geese block. Sew one on either side of the second block. Set aside.

6 Place the 3 ½" (9cm) green square with a white 4 ¼" (11cm) square with right sides facing lining it up to one corner. Sew along the drawn line and trim the excess fabric to ¼" (0.6cm).

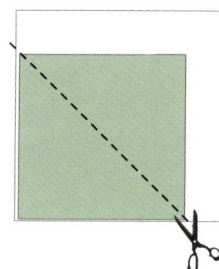

7 Fold the triangle down and press the seam to the green fabric.

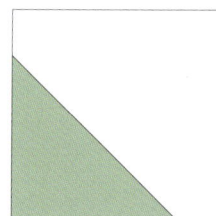

8 Now sew these pieces together by first sewing on the flying geese piece with only one white square. Then sew on the other piece to the top. Press seams towards the large white square.

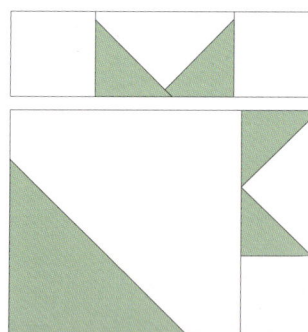

9 Sew the larger flying geese pieces in the same way as the smaller ones. For each block you will need 4 - 3" (8cm) squares and 2 - 3" x 5 ½" (8 x 14cm) white rectangles.

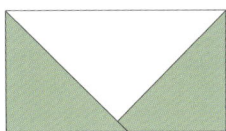

10 Once they are sewn and pressed, sew a 3 ½" (9cm) half square triangle to the right side of one of the flying geese piece.

11 Sew the large flying geese block to the right side of the block and then the other piece to the top.

Press the seams towards the flying geese.

Repeat these steps to make 8 blocks.

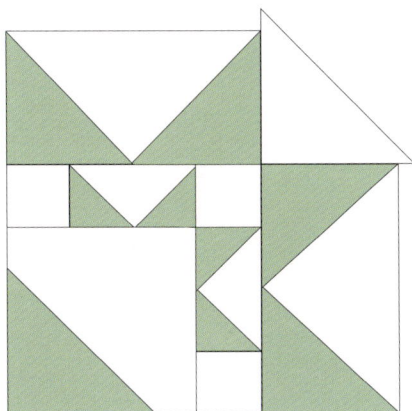

12 Lay them out as desired or as shown.

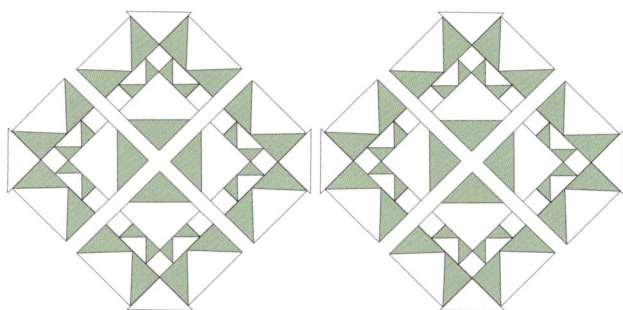

13 Sew a 1 ¾" (4.5cm) strip to the centre of 2 blocks as shown. Trim as needed. Sew another strip to either side of the connected blocks to make one large star block. Trim the excess strip as needed.

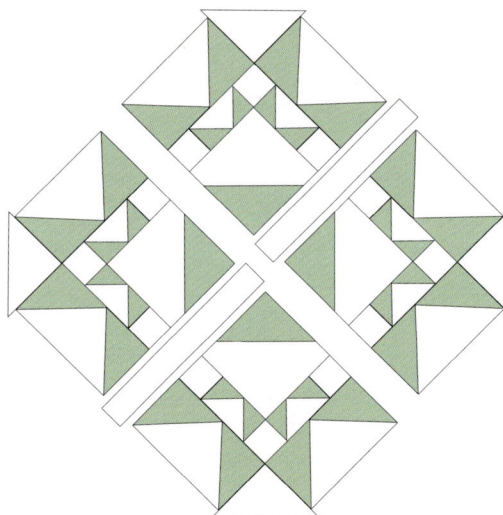

14 Sew a 3 ½" (9cm) triangle to the one corner. Sew the 8 ½" (22cm) triangles to the opposite side. Sew a 1 ¾" (4.5cm) strip in the centre.

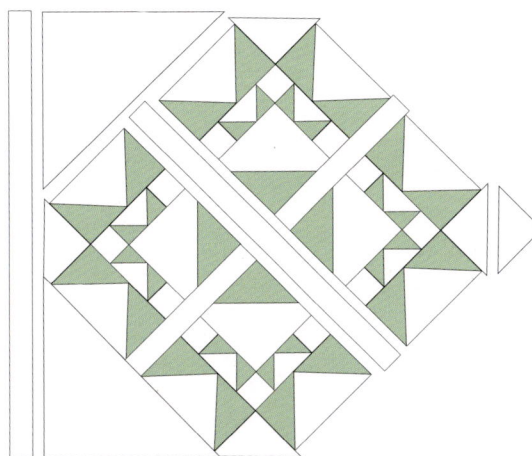

15 Join both large blocks. Press well.

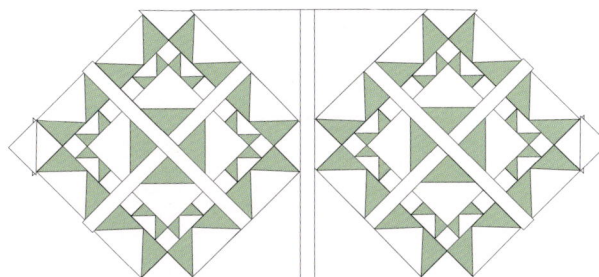

16 Layer with batting and backing. Press, pin and then quilt as desired. Trim the edges leaving at least ¼" (0.6cm) from all points.

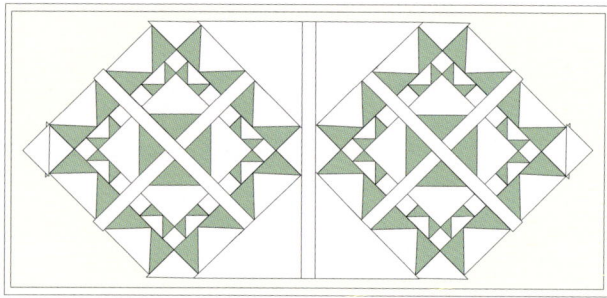

For the binding, cut 3 – 2" (5cm) strips

17 Please note; the following diagrams are only showing one 60° corner. Using a ¼" (0.6cm) seam, sew on the binding with the right side down of the runner. Stop sewing when you are ¼" (0.6cm) from the corner.

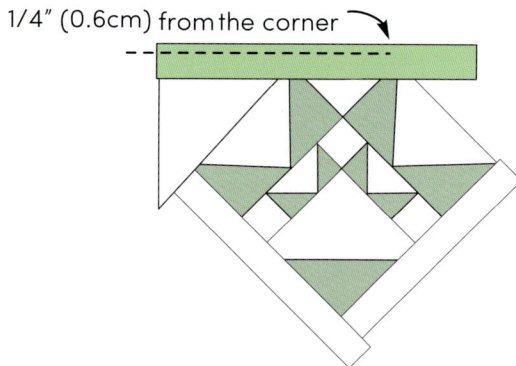

1/4" (0.6cm) from the corner

18 Lift presser foot, and with the needle up, turn the quilt. Keeping the thread attached in the machine, fold binding up as shown.

Lining up with the angle of the quilt.

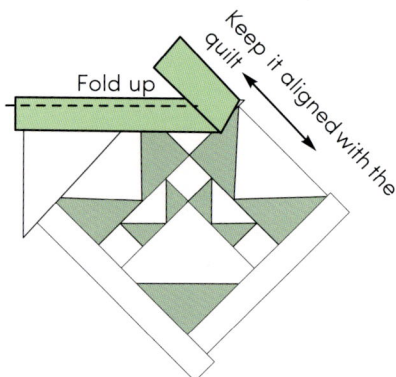

Fold up

Keep it aligned with the quilt

19 Now fold the binding down, and continue to sew a ¼" (0.6cm) seam along the border.

Repeat for the 45° corners.

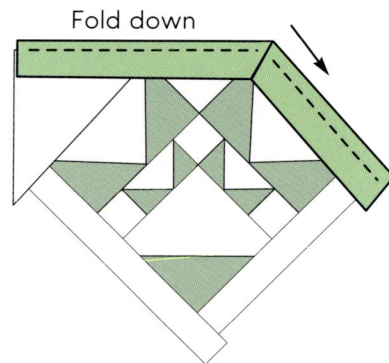

Fold down

20 Fold binding to the back and tuck under ¼" (0.6cm). Handstitch with small slip stitches. Fold corners in to create a 60° angle so they duplicate the front corners.

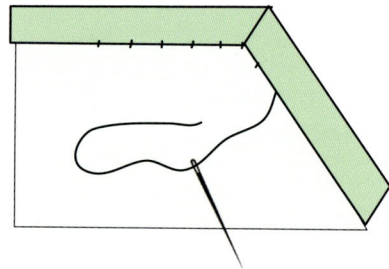

STRAWBERRY STAR

This beatiful collection of strawberry fabrics whisks me back to dreamy days as a little girl playing with my Strawberry Shortcake dolls. These stars have danced their way from my childhood and landed right onto this quilt. I love how memories weave themselves into each pattern I create.

Finished Measurements
37" x 37" (94 x 94cm)

Materials Needed

❋ 4" x 42" (10 x 107cm) Strips of fabric from 6 different prints

❋ 4" x 42" (10 x 107cm) Strips of fabric from 6 different low volume prints

❋ 1.1 Yards (1m) of backing

❋ 39" x 39" (99 x 99cm) Piece of thin batting

❋ Matching thread

CUTTING

From the pink fabrics cut;
36 – 4" (10cm) squares
20 – 3 ½" (9cm) squares

From the low volume fabrics cut;
34 – 4" (10cm) squares
54 – 3 ½" (9cm) squares

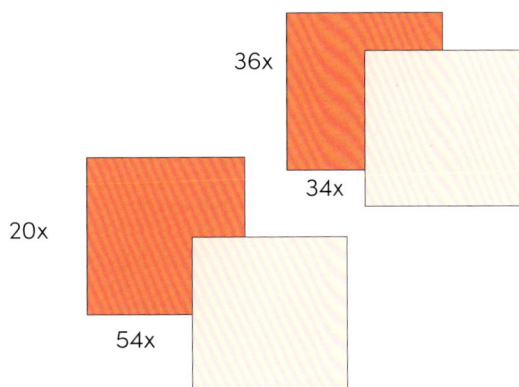

36x

34x

20x

54x

1 With the 34 low volume and 1 pink 4" (10cm) squares, using a pen draw a line diagonally from corner to corner on the wrong side of each piece.

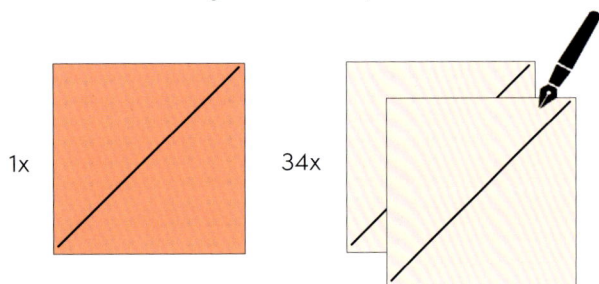

1x

34x

2 Layer the low volume squares with the pink squares right sides facing and sew a ¼" (0.6cm) seam on either side of the drawn line. You can do this by chain piecing to save time.

Cut them along the line. Trim the squares to 3 ½" (9cm).

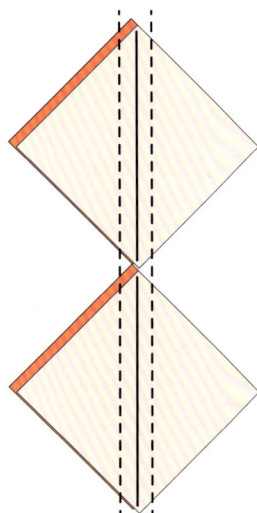

PRESSING

3 Using a hot iron, press the seams towards the pink fabric by following the arrows as shown. Push the iron towards the centre first, and then press the seams on either side. This will help the pieces to maintain their shape.

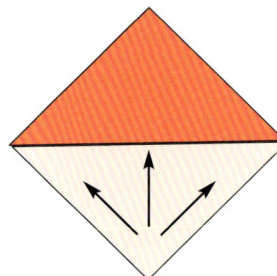

4 Lay out the pieces in the order shown. There are 2 pink half square triangles and they are outlined in the diagram below.

Gather your pieces and sew them in rows and then sew the rows together. Allow the seams to fall in the direction they most naturally go, but still butting them up against each other.

Press. Layer with the backing and batting and quilt as desired.

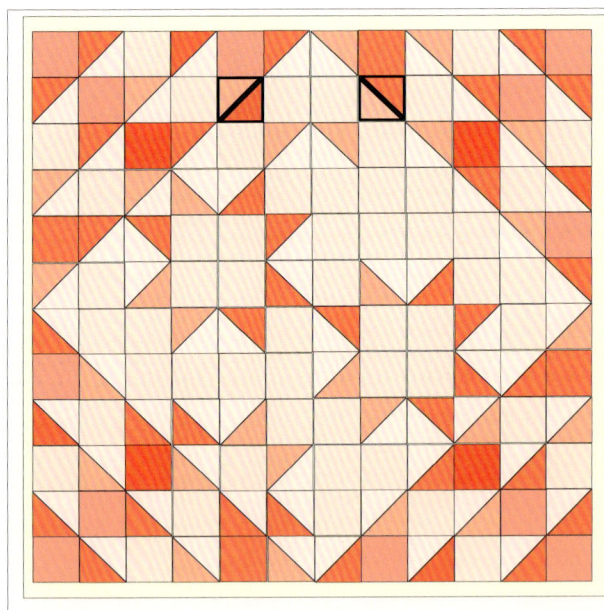

5 Cut 4 strips 2" (5cm) x WOF. Sew them together at the ends. Bind quilt using the instructions on page 10.

DRESDEN FLOWER MUG RUG

Having tea? Need a drop spot for your phone? A gift for a teacher? Put down your tea and look no further. This mug rug is perfect little project to practice my techniques to perfect your Dresden making skills.

Finished Measurements
10" (25.5cm) in Diameter

Materials Needed

✳ 10 – 2 ½" (6cm) Squares fabrics

✳ 6" (15cm) Square for centre

✳ 2 – 12" (30.5cm) Squares for background and backing

✳ 1 ½" (3.6cm) Bias strip x 30" (76cm) long

✳ 2" (5cm) Piece of ribbon (if desired)

✳ 12" Square of fusible batting

✳ Matching sewing thread

CUTTING & SEWING

1 Cut your scrap pieces of 2 ½" (6cm) squares into 10 pieces from the template on page 109.

2 Reduce your stitch length on your sewing machine to 1.8.

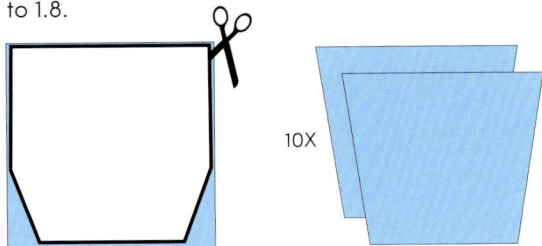

10X

3 Fold the first piece with right sides together lengthwise. Sew across the wide end with a ¼" (0.6cm) seam. Continue to sew the remaining pieces using chain stitching. (You do not cut the thread, and continue to sew the pieces.) When you are finished, clip them apart.

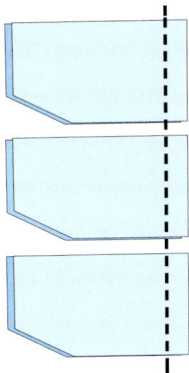

4 Using your scissors, gently turn the ends right side out to create a point. (This will make each piece look like an arrow.) Line up the seam directly in the centre of each blade and finger press the "point".

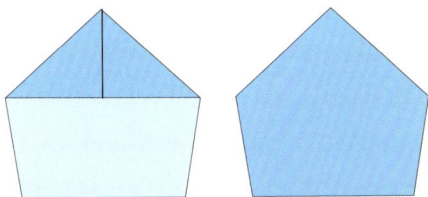

5 Place two blades together with right sides facing, lining up the points. Sew a ¼" seam along the edge. Fold the seams to the left after each dresden plate is sewn. Continue to sew on each plate in the same way. When you have them all sewn on, then sew the first one and last one together to make a circle.

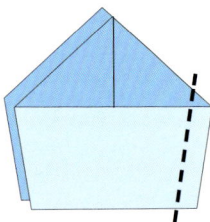

6 Once your Dresden is sewn, turn over with right side down onto the ironing board.

Press the seams in the same direction. As you are pressing, gently pull the blades so they are flat.

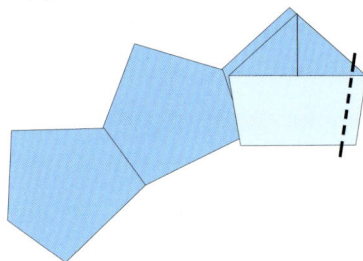

7 Flip the Dresden over with right side facing up. You may need to carefully move the blades to position them so there is a perfect circle in the centre.

Lightly spray with water and press well.

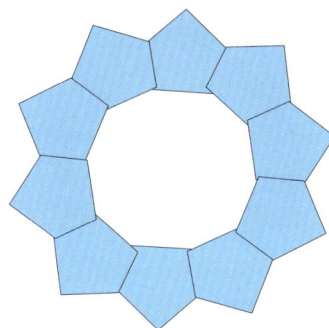

8 Layer the backing, batting and background fabric. Place the Dresden in the center. Put tiny dabs of glue under each blade, reposition and then press into place.

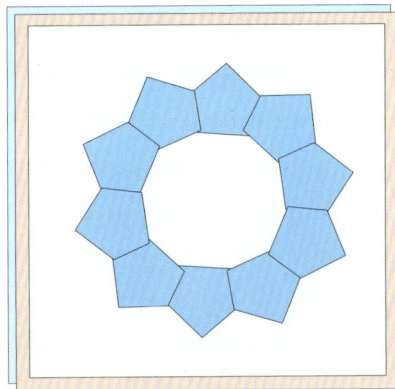

9 Cut out the circle template from cardstock from page 109. A cracker or cereal box works well for this. If you are "fussy cutting" out a design from the fabric, you may want to put the circle behind the fabric to see if it will fit into the circle shape. This can help you decide if the circle is the right size.

10 Place onto your centre fabric and cut around the circle ¼" - ⅜" (0.6 - 1cm) larger than the template.

With a needle and thread, make a tiny gathering stitches ⅛" (0.3cm) from the edge of the circle.

11 Pull the gather tightly. You can even pull it so that the cardstock bends up slightly. It will relax once you have tied a knot in the end. Press well.

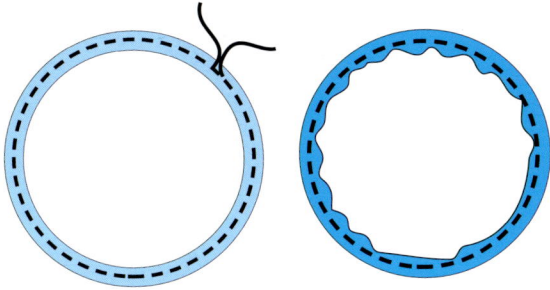

12 Once it is cooled, carefully remove the cardstock circle. Press again. Place the circle right side up and put tiny dabs of clue all the way around the gathering edge.

13 Position circle on top of Dresden just letting it 'rest' there. Use a ruler if needed to be sure it is in the centre. Using the iron, press it once quickly, then check the position again before pressing it well.

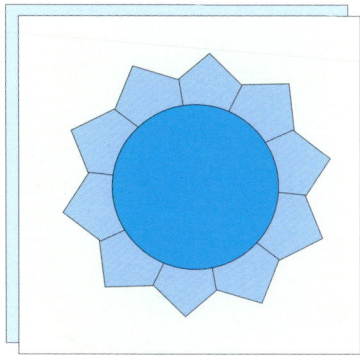

14 Cut out the outer circle template and place it on top of the Dresden. You may find it helpful to fold the circle template in half, and then in half again, and centering it on the Dresden centre. Trace around the outer edge.

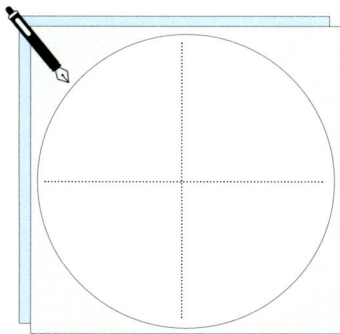

15 Hand stitch the Dresden and centre in place using a sewing machine, zig-zag stitch, buttonhole stitch, or other decorative stitch.

16 Pin through all layers close to the traced outer line. Sew slowly directly on the line gently smoothing the fabric towards the outer edges while you sew. You will find it can buckle and pull.

Cut ⅛" (0.3cm) around the outer edge of the circle.

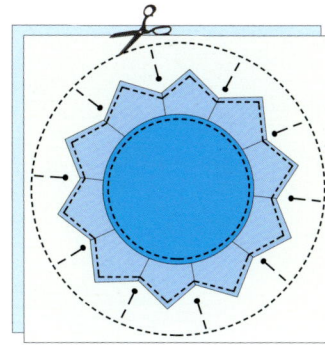

BINDING

1 Cut a strip of binding on the bias, 30" (76cm) long - 1 ½" (3.8cm) wide from the binding fabric.

2 Using a ¼" (0.6cm) seam, sew it on while gently turning the circle and **without pulling and stretching the binding.**

Gently "feed" the binding while you sew. If you pull the binding it will create a "bowl" shape with your circle.

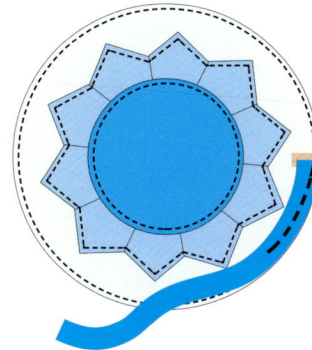

3 When you get to the end.... Fold over the beginning end of the binding and lay the end on top of it. Continue to sew the ends.

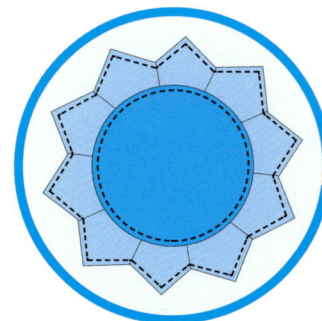

Or; You can use a small piece of ribbon and lay it down first where the seams will meet, then cut off the binding when you reach the ribbon. This will make less bulk at the seam. Fold ribbon and binding over and sew as in following steps.

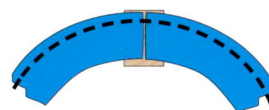

SEW MUCH LOVE PILLOW

Tiny pieces of miniature prints lovingly pieced together into simple little hearts beautifully manifest the expression of love.

Finished Measurements
18" (45.5cm) Square

Materials Needed

✳ As many different prints as you would like to use. Each piece should measure no less than 1 ½" (3.8cm) square – (204 in total)

✳ As many different low volume (white) fabrics as you would like to use. Each piece should measure no less than 1 ½" (3.8cm) square – (216 in total)

✳ 1 Fat quarter for lining

✳ 1 Fat quarter for backing

✳ ⅛ Yard (0.1m) for binding (dark pink)

✳ 20" x 20" (51 x 51cm) Piece of thin batting

✳ 1 – 22" (56cm) Zipper

✳ 20" (51cm) Pillow form

✳ Matching sewing thread

CUTTING

Cut 204 – 1 ½" (3.8cm) squares from your scrap stash.

Cut 216 – 1 ½" (3.8cm) squares from low volume white prints.

You will need to make 96 half square triangles. Randomly select from the low volume and scrappy squares.

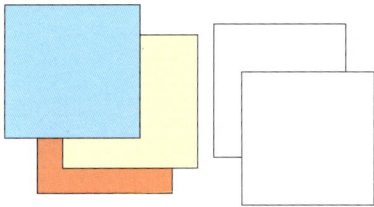

1 Layer the white (low volume square) and scrappy square with right sides facing. Sew from corner to corner at an angle.

Hint: You may wish to use a piece of tape to mark your sewing machine so that you can guide these pieces in a straight line without marking them.

Continue to chain piece the 96 half square triangles.

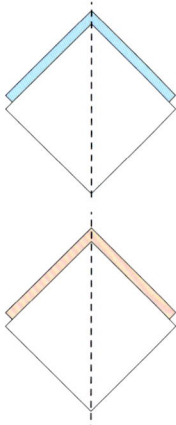

2 Cut the pieces apart and trim off one side leaving at least a ¼" (0.6cm) seam.

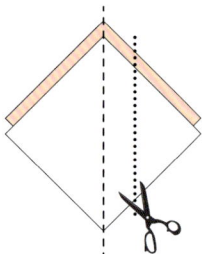

3 Press the seams towards the scrappy fabric.

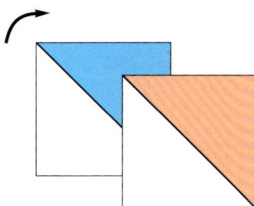

4 Following the piecing diagram (#17), gather the pieces randomly and sew them together using a ¼" (0.6cm) seam.

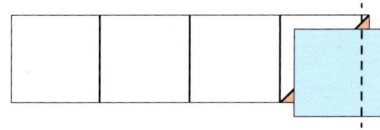

5 You may want to number each row to keep track which peices need to be sewn next.

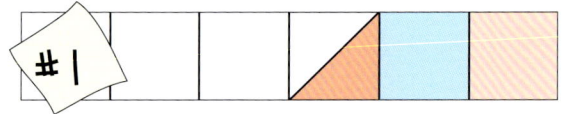

6 Sew each row together once it has been sewn, then start the next row.

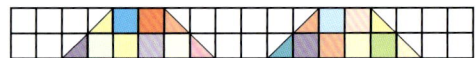

7 Continue to sew the remaining rows.

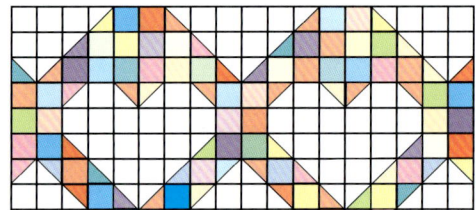

Tips For Sewing Small:

• Only press your seams after each row is sewn. This way you can adjust any seams if needed before they are set.

• You may wish to use a sharp tool (small pair of scissors) to help guide your small pieces into the sewing machine as you go.

• Try to "butt up your seams" if possible, but don't worry if there are some that don't.

8 Once the top is complete, layer with batting and lining and quilt as desired.

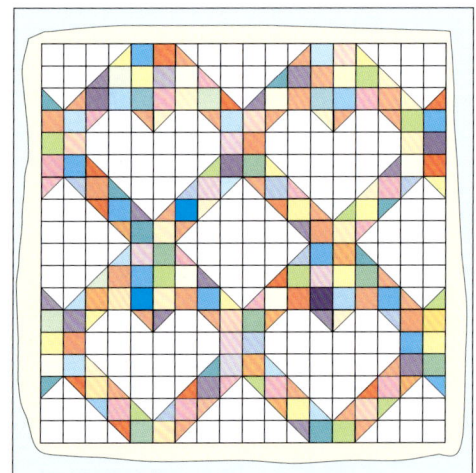

9 To sew on the zipper, use the backing fat quarter and lay it **right side up** and zipper **right side down** along the salvage edge.

You may need to place it about 1" (2.5cm) from the edge so that the sewing covers the salvage. This is used so that you do not need to finish this edge. Sew the zipper on along the zipper tape.

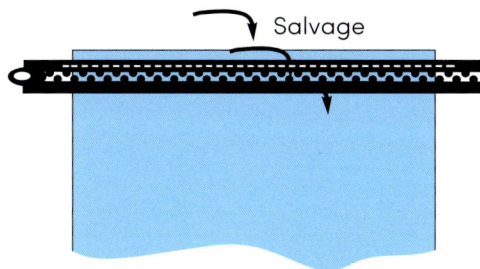

Salvage

10 Fold the fabric to cover the zipper teeth and half of the zipper tape. This will make a "lip" to hide the zipper. Pin in place and then press.

Sew a seam along the layers through the zipper tape to hold it in place.

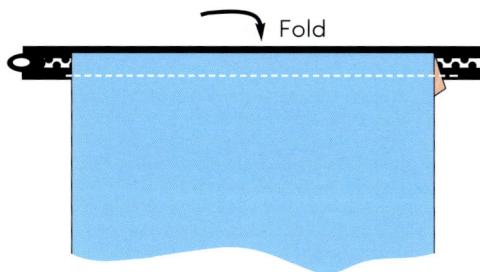

Fold

11 Take your pillow front and flip it over so the wrong side is facing you and the pillow bottom is at the top. (I prefer to have the zipper at the bottom of the pillow but you may want it on the side or top, it is up to you.)

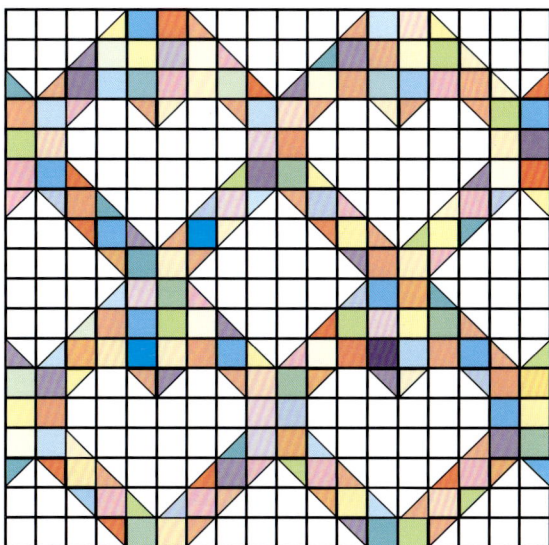

12 Line up the zipper ⅛" (0.3cm) from the edge of the pillow. Sew the zipper on along the zipper tape. Be sure you do not catch the "lip" in the sewing. You can pull it down and pin it if needed.

Open the zipper half way before sewing on the binding. You may need to move the zipper pull open and closed as you sew it on to keep it out of the way.

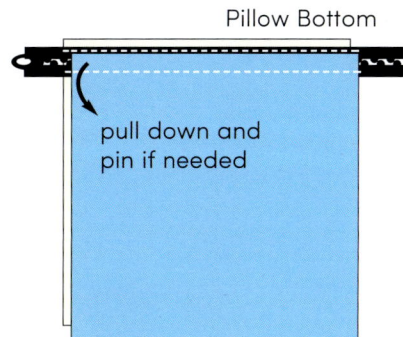

Pillow Bottom

pull down and pin if needed

For the binding, cut two- 2 ½" x 42" (6.5 x 107cm) strips.

Please Note: the following diagrams are only showing one corner of the pillow.

13 Fold the binding in half legthwise with wrong sides together.

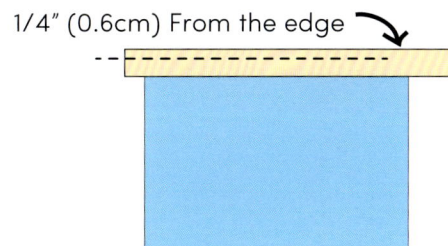

1/4" (0.6cm) From the edge

14 Using a ⅜" (1cm) seam, sew on the binding with the right side down, starting at the bottom of the pillow back. Stop sewing when you are ¼" (0.6cm) from the corner. Lift presser foot and turn the quilt.

Keeping the thread attached in the machine, fold binding up as shown.

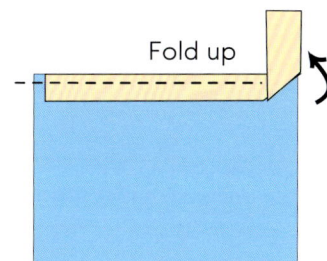

Fold up

15 Now fold the binding down, and continue to sew a ¼" (0.6cm) seam along the border.

Repeat for all corners.

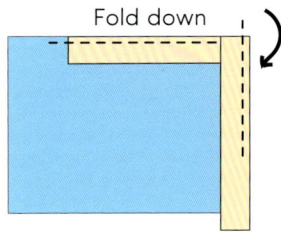

Fold down

16 Fold binding to the front and topstitch along the seam edge. Fold corners in to create a 45° angle

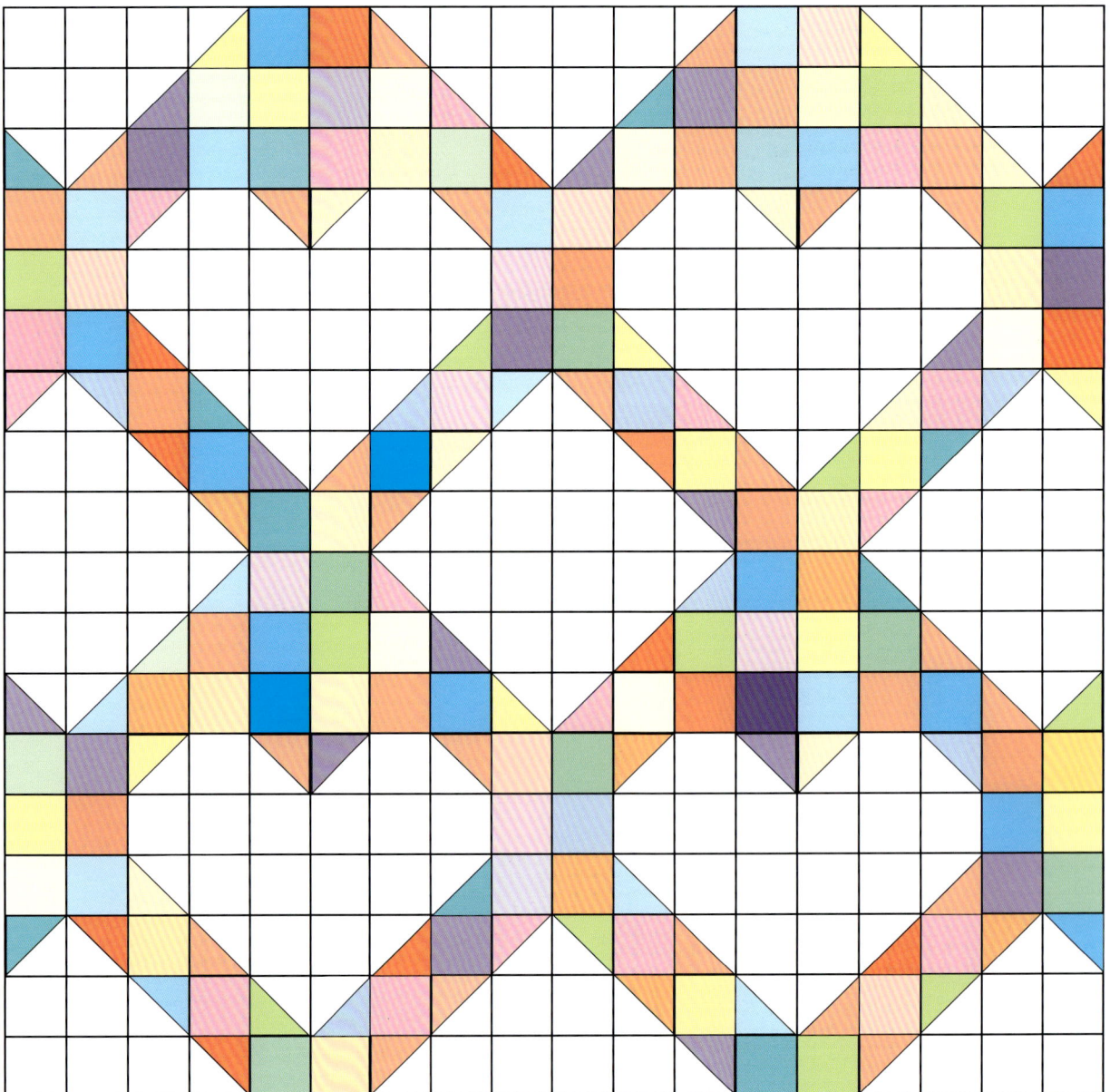

so they duplicate the front corners and be sure you do not sew over the zipper lip.

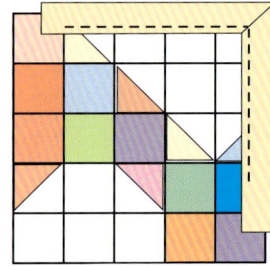

Piecing Diagram

HEXIE PINCUSHION

This sweet hexie pincushion is all about the buzz. Combine your newly acquired paper-piecing skills and bright yellow fabrics to complete this nature inspired gift for that sewing friend who you think has it all. Well, now they do!

Finished Measurements
4" Wide x 1 ½" Tall (10 x 3.8cm)

Materials Needed

✳ Various pieces of yellow fabric measuring
1" x 2" (2.5 x 5cm) to 1" x 4" (2.5 x 10cm)

✳ 6" x 6" (15 x 15cm) Piece for the pincushion bottom

✳ Polyfil

✳ Matching sewing thread

HEXIE PINCUSHION

1 Paper Piece the top of the pinchushion using the paper piecing instructions from page 8.

To create the look of the yellow and white alternating, you will need to sew the colors in three's. For example. Sew 2, 3 & 4 with white fabric. 5, 6, & 7 with yellow fabric. It can be helpful to colour the template so you can keep track of the order of the colours.

Trim the outer edges if needed.

2 Layer the front and base hexie of the pincushion with right sides facing and thin batting on top of the base fabric.

3 Sew a ¼" (0.6cm) seam around the edges leaving a small opening on one side. Be sure to stitch past the corners and then backstitch at the ends.

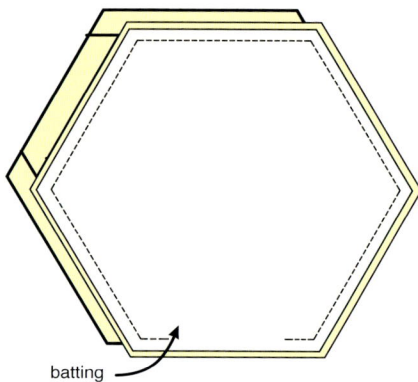

batting

4 Pinch the corners so that the side seams match and sew across each corner.

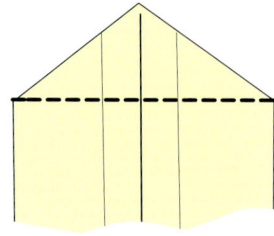

5 Carefully turn right side out and fill with fiber fill.

6 Ladder stitch the opening closed.

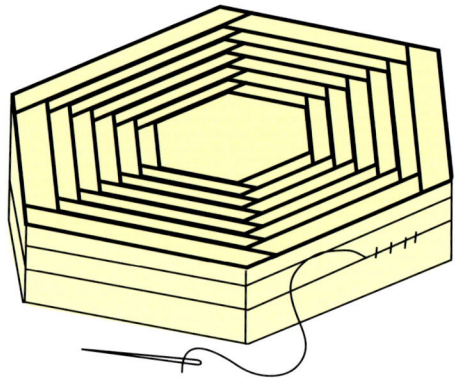

TABLET CASE

Pink is always my first choice for fabric colours. Bubblegum and velvet soft rosebuds, icing on a birthday cake, and cozy pajamas. Choose your favourite colour scheme and wrap that comfort and security around your handy device.

Finished Measurements
10" x 13" (25.5 x 33cm)

Materials Needed

✳ 12 Strips of fabric from light to dark measuring
1 ½" x 42" (3.8 x 107cm) long

✳ 2 Strips of pink fabric measuring 1 ½" x 42" (3.8 x 107cm)
long for binding

✳ Pink lining fabric measuring 14" x 22" (35.5 x 56cm)

✳ Thin batting 14" x 22" (35.5 x 56cm)

✳ 3 Pieces of white low volume fabric 4" x 5" (10 x 13cm)

✳ 1 – 14" (35.5cm) Zipper

✳ Matching sewing thread

Lay out your strips to create an ombre look from dark to light to dark. Once you are happy with the order of the fabrics, label them #1 to #12 to keep them in order. You will need to cut out pieces from color 3, 4, 6, 7, 9 & 10.

From these strips cut;
• 1 – 1 ¼" x 3" (3 x 8cm)
• 1 – 1 ½" x 1 ½" (3.8 x 3.8cm)
• 2 – 1 ½" x 2 ½" (3.8 x 6cm)
• 1 – 1 ½" x 11 ¼" (3.8 x 28.5cm)

From the strips marked 1, 2, 5, 8, 11 & 12 cut;
• 1 – 1 ½" x 8 ½" (3.8 x 22cm)
• 1 – 1 ½" x 11 ¼" (3.8 x 28.5cm)

From each of the low volume prints cut;
• 1 – 1 ½" x 2 ½" (3.8 x 6.5cm)
• 1 – 1 ¼" x 3 ½" (3 x 9cm)

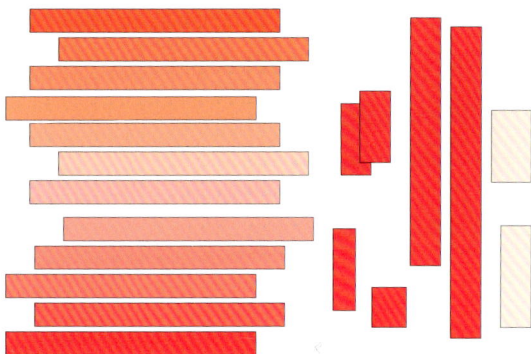

1 On each of the pink 1 ½" (3.8cm) squares draw a line with a pen or pencil diagonally on the wrong side of the squares.

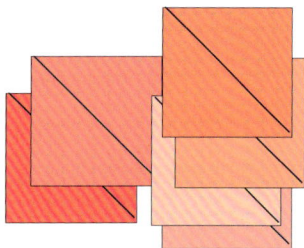

SEWING

2 Gather the #3 and #4 pink pieces. Be very careful to keep them organized while sewing the arrows.

3 With the pink #3 square, position onto the left side of the white (or low volume print) 1 ½" x 2 ½" (3.8 x 6.5cm) rectangle with right sides together. Sew it directly along the drawn line. Trim the seam to ¼" (0.6cm) and fold the piece back and finger press with the seams towards the pink triangle.

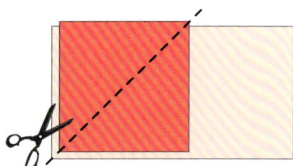

Tips: These pieces are very small, so having a new sewing machine needle can be helpful.

Begin sewing the middle top edge to the corner rather than from the corner to avoid the corner fabrics getting caught in the sewing machine.

4 Position the #4 pink square onto the right side and sew along the drawn line. Trim.

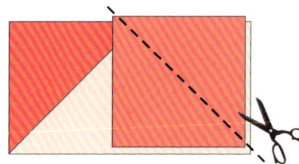

5 To press your tiny "flying geese" piece, it can be helpful to iron straight towards the centre tip and then to either side at the middle of each triangle. This can prevent the triangles from becoming distorted and maintain it's shape.

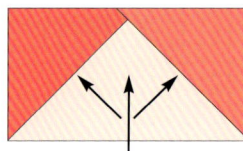

6 Sew the #3 1 ¼" x 3" (3 x 8cm) piece to the left side of the white rectangle. Sew the #4 piece to the right side.

7 Press seams towards the pink pieces.

8 Sew the remainder #3 and #4 rectangles together in pairs. Press.

x2

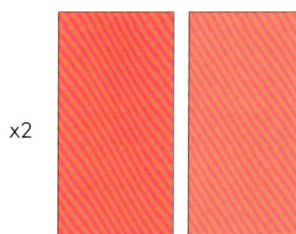

9 Sew the arrow pieces together as shown.

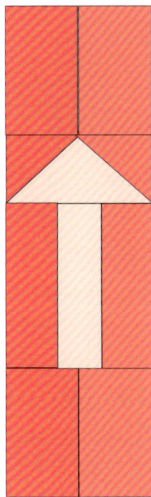

10 Repeat these steps with the pieces marked #6 and #7, then #9 and #10.

11 Lay out the 8 ½" (22cm) pink strips in the numerical order including the arrow pieces. Sew them all together then press with seams in the same direction.

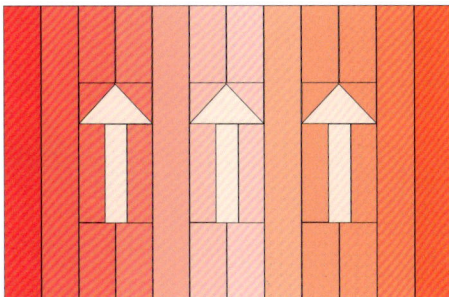

12 Lay out the 11 ¼" (28.5cm) strips in numerical order and sew them together. Press the seams in the same direction.

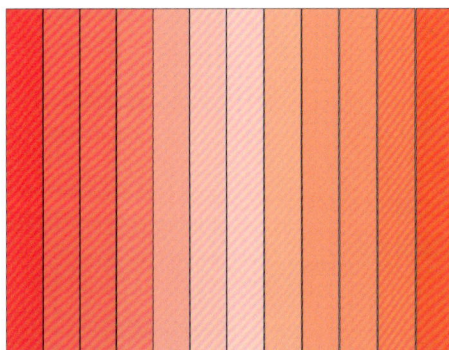

13 Layer the lining (inside of the case) with the fusible batting and place the case front and back on top. Press the layers together.

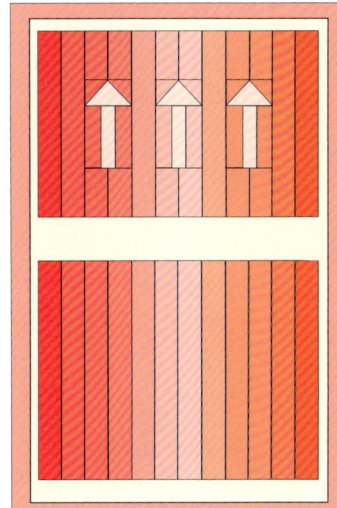

Tip: You may want to place parchment paper on top to protect your iron from the fusible batting.

14 Quilt layers together as desired. Trim the front and back pieces.

15 Sew on the binding strip along the case edges.

Be sure to match up the ombre strips as shown.

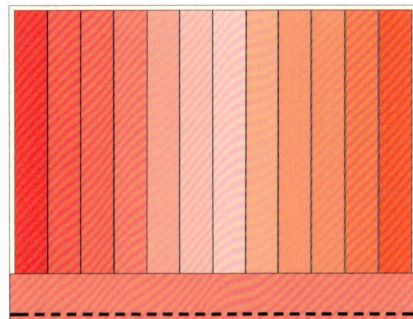

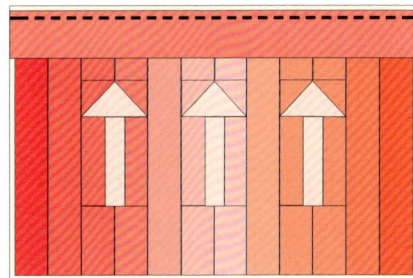

16 Fold the binding strip over and under and press. Sew the zipper lining up the teeth along the binding edge.

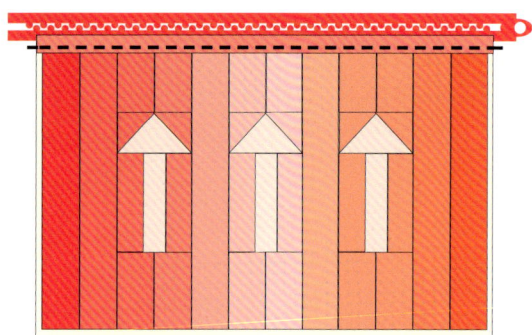

17 Cut a piece 12" (30.5cm) long from the binding strip. Fold lengthwise with right sides facing and sew together with a ¼" (0.6cm) seam. Turn rught side out and press.

18 Fold the handle in half and pin it in place on top of the zipper at the right side of the case. Open the zipper halfway to keep the zipper pull out of the way.

19 Stitch it in place to hold the zipper and handle.

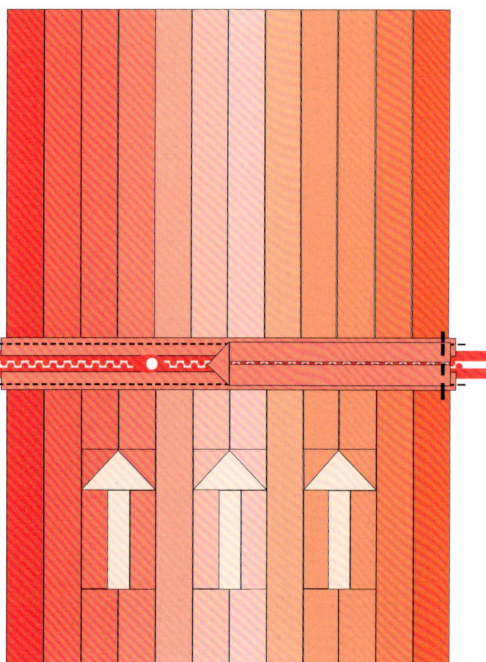

20 Fold the back of the case down matching up the side and bottom edges. Pin them in place.

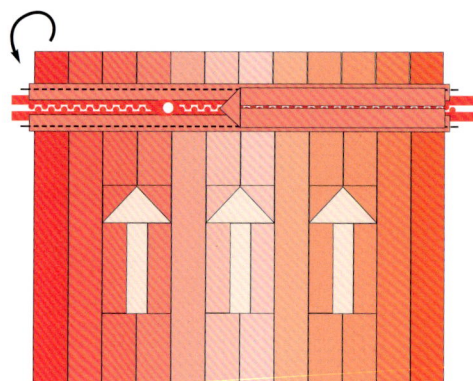

21 Flip the case over to the back. Sew the binding strip right side down leaving about ½" (1.3cm) overhang at the top. When you reach the corner, stop sewing ¼" (0.6cm) from the corner.

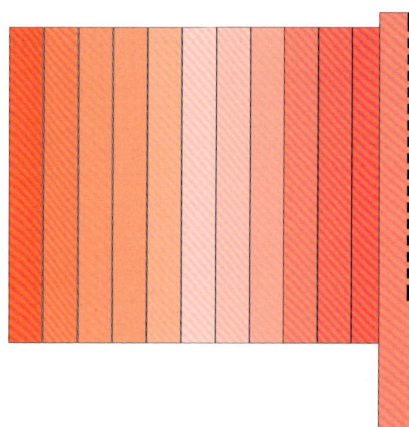

22 Fold the binding up to make a 45° angle.

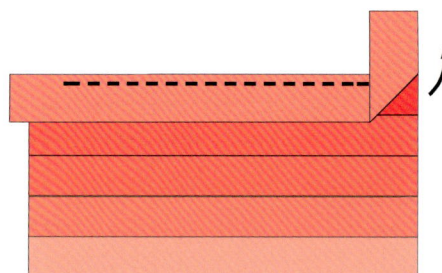

23 Fold the binding down lining up the fold with the corner edge. Continue to sew on the binding and repeat for the second corner.

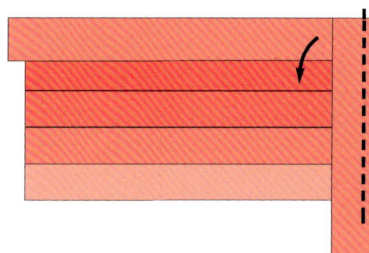

48

24 Trim the binding at the top of the case leaving ½" (1.3cm) overhang.

25 Flip the case over to the front and fold the ½" (1.3cm) binding edge down, then fold the binding twice. Topstitch it in place with matching thread. Backstitch at either end.

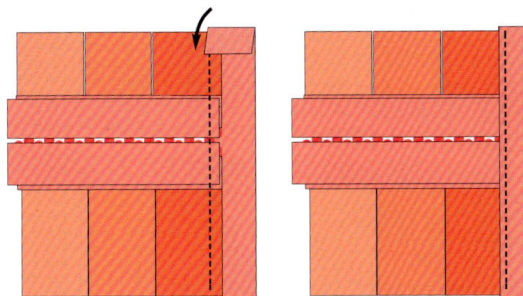

MINT ANGLE POUCH

Ready to embrace the tide of gratitude from friends and family for whom you sew this for? The dimensional design that sets this pouch apart is on point. You've got this one in the bag.

Finished Measurements
8" Tall x 9" Wide x 4" Deep (20.5 x 23 x 10cm)

Materials Needed

✳ 32 – 2" x 5" (5 x 13cm) Various green fabric pieces

✳ 14" x 24" (35.5 x 61cm) Piece of thin batting

✳ ½ Yard (0.45m) of cotton lining and trim

✳ ⅓ Yard (0.3m) of low volume fabric for pouch front and side

✳ 1 – 14" (35.5cm) Zipper

✳ Matching sewing thread

1 Using the template from page 108, paper piece 4 sections for the pouch sides.

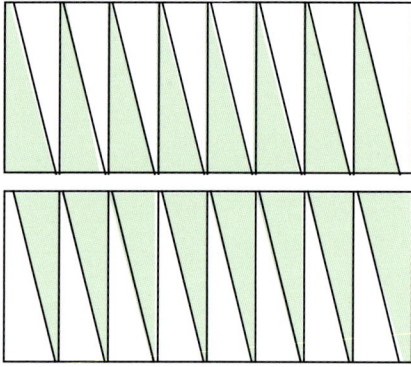

2 Remove the papers, and press. Sew 2 sections together for each side.

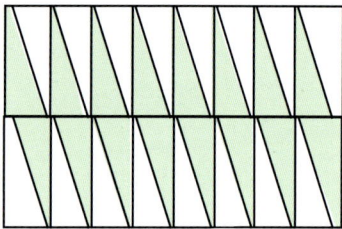

3 Cut the side pouch piece (if you haven't already done so) to measure 4" x 21" (10 x 53.5cm) long.

4 Layer the pouch pieces with batting and the inside lining fabric. Pin to hold them in place.

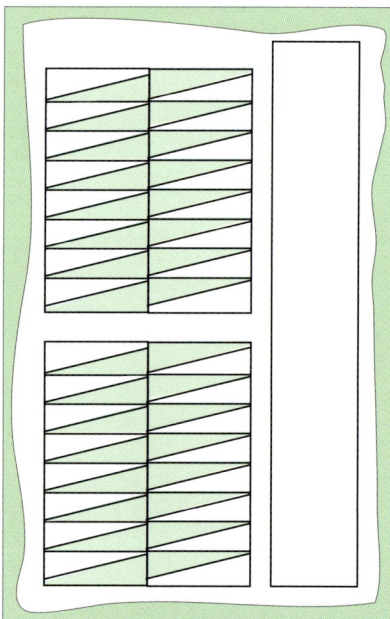

5 Machine sew layers together. This can be any pattern or quilting technique. Use the same quilting on the two side pieces.

6 Cut the pieces from the lining.

7 Cut 2 pieces measuring 1 ½" x 4" (3.8 x 10cm) from the lining or trim fabric.

8 Finish the ends of the 21" (53.5cm) side strip by sewing it to the back with right sides facing with a ¼" (0.6cm) seam.

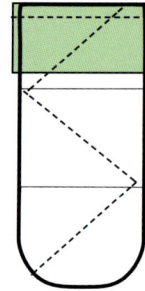

9 Fold it down and over to the front and topstitch it along the edge.

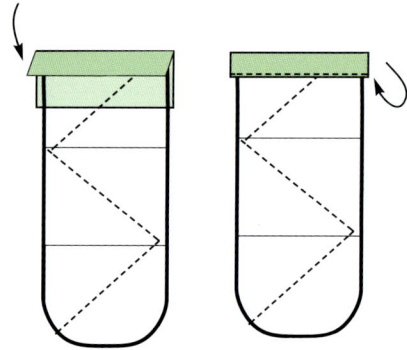

10 Cut the corners of the pouch using the pouch side template.

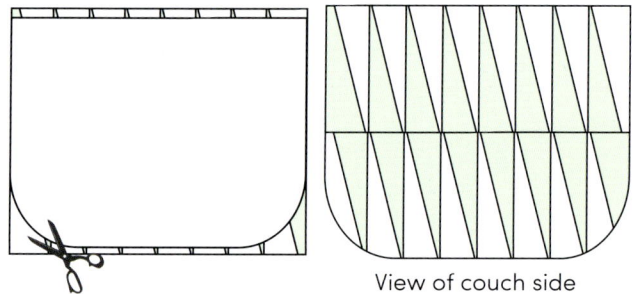

View of couch side

11 Mark the center of the pouch bottom and the center of the side strip. Using quilt clips or pins, begin pinning from the center to either side.

12 Sew the side strip to the bag using a ¼" (0.6cm) seam. Turn the bag while sewing, being careful not to bunch up the fabric on the side strip or the pouch as you sew.

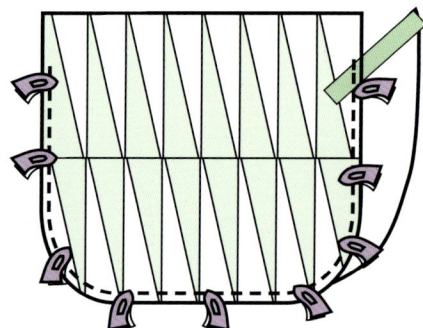

13 Do the same for the opposite side.

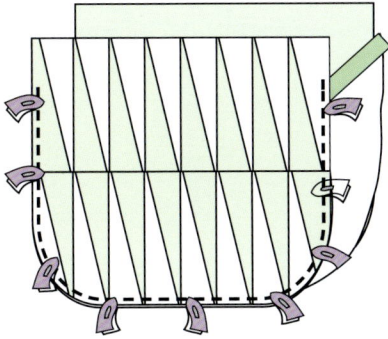

14 Cut 2 binding strips measuring 1 ¾" x 42" (4.5 x 107cm).

15 With a strip of the 1 ¾" (4.5cm) edge fabric, place it right side down lining up with the top of the bag and right side facing the side strip piece. Sew it on using a seam slightly bigger than a ¼" (0.6cm) seam. This will cover your previous stitches. Sew it around to the opposite side.

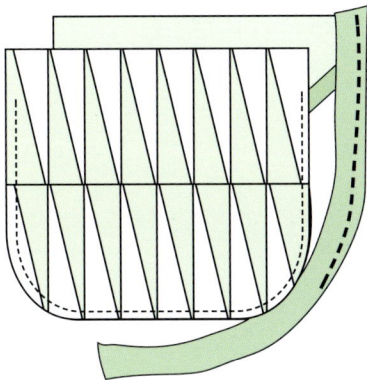

16 Turn the binding over and under and handstitch it down to the front of the pouch using very small stitches.

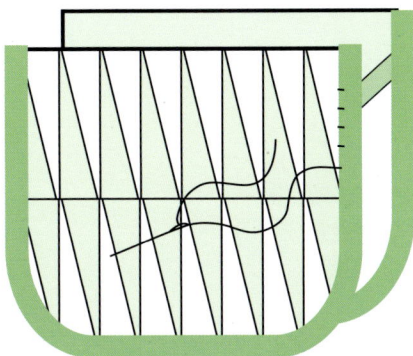

ZIPPER

18 Start by pinning the zipper (right side up) at the open end of the zipper. Pin the zipper ½" (1.3cm)

from the end at the inside of the bag, folding up the end of the zipper under at 45° angle.

Continue to pin it in place until you reach the other end of the bag. You will need to leave at least 4" (10cm) hanging over the end of the bag. If your zipper is long and you have more than 3" (8cm) hanging over, that is fine, you can trim it off later.

19 Sew it on using a ¼" (0.6cm) seam. Sew it to the end of the bag and backstitch. Do the same for the opposite side of the zipper.

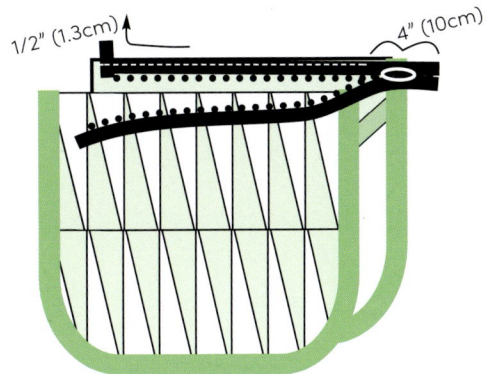

1/2" (1.3cm)   4" (10cm)

20 With the binding strip, line it up on the inside of the bag on top of the zipper with right side down. Fold the end ½" (1.3cm) as shown, and sew it on using a ¼" (0.6cm) seam.

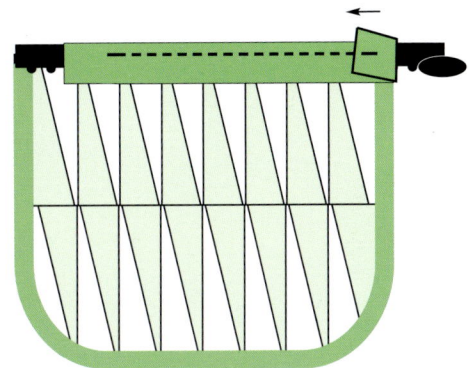

21 Sew the binding to the end of the bag, then leave 10" (25.5cm) of binding, then start sewing the binding on the opposite side. When you reach the end, be sure to trim the binding, and fold the end in just as you did when you started sewing the binding on. (Like when you began sewing it on the opposite side.)

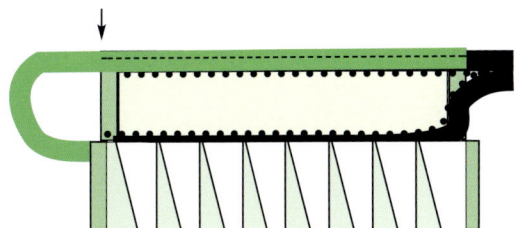

22 Fold the binding over and sew in place using a ¼" (0.6cm) seam around the entire binding edge, including the 10" (25.5cm) loop. Backstitch at the beginning and end.

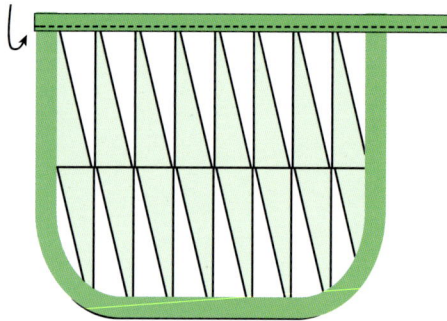

23 Close the zipper. Trim the zipper so that it is 4" (10cm) from the edge of the bag.

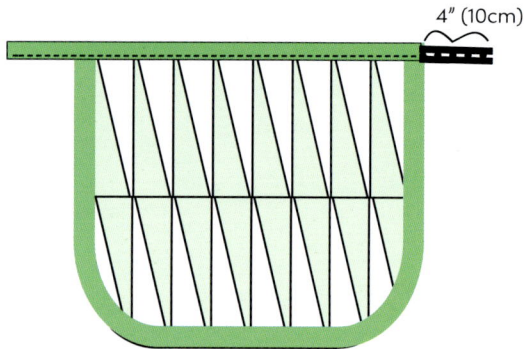

4" (10cm)

24 To sew on the zipper end, cut off a 1 ½" (3.8cm) piece from the binding strip.

25 Place the piece under the zipper with right side facing up. Sew on with a ¼" (0.6cm) seam.

26 Fold the fabric end down and then fold the sides into the centre.

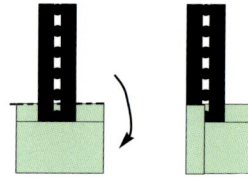

27 Fold the end up, and then again, hiding all seams. Hand stitch the end down with small stitches.

RAINBOW PRISM WALL HANGING

This showstopper will stop you in your tracks. A delightful mix of rainbow colours that twinkle and sparkle in the sunshine all year round. No sunshine required for even the rainiest of days.

Finished Measurements
22 ½" (57cm) Square

Materials Needed

✳ 6 – 2 ½" (6.5cm) Squares in purple fabrics

✳ 12 – 2 ½" (6.5cm) Squares in blue fabrics

✳ 6 – 2 ½" (6.5cm) Squares in green fabrics

✳ 6 – 2 ½" (6.5cm) Squares in yellow fabrics

✳ 12 – 2 ½" (6.5cm) Squares in orange fabrics

✳ 6 – 2 ½" (6.5cm) Squares in pink fabrics

✳ Fabric pieces that measure at least 2 ¼" x 3 ½" (5.5 x 9cm) (The Dresden Blades) 7 Purple, 7 Blue, 14 Green, 14 Yellow, 7 Orange, 7 Pink

✳ 4 Different fat quarters of low volume prints

✳ 2" x 10" (5 x 25.5cm) – 20" (51cm) Pieces for binding

✳ Matching sewing thread

✳ 24" x 24" (61 x 61cm) of Thin batting

CUTTING

From each of the 2 ¼" x 3 ½" (5.5 x 9cm) pieces cut out Dresden blades from the template on page 110.

From each of the white or low volume print cut;

3 – 6" (15cm) squares

1 – 6 ½" (16.5cm) square cut into 2 triangles

2 – 2 ½" x 4 ½" (6.5 x 11.5cm) rectangles

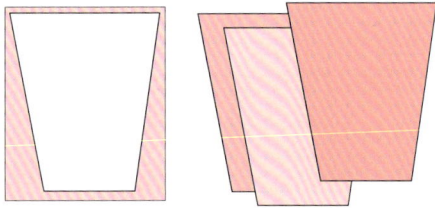

1   Prepare the 2 ½" (6.5cm) squares for sewing by using a pen and ruler and draw a diagonal line from corner to corner on the wrong side of the fabric. You will need to do this to;

2 pink squares
4 orange
2 yellow
2 green
4 blue
2 purple

2   It will be helpful to lay out your low volume pieces to be sure that each of the patterns are evenly spaced before you begin to sew. You can choose they layout you like best.

This also includes the 2 ½" x 4 ½" (6.5 x 11.5cm) rectangles so they match up with the half square triangles that are sewn to the same block.

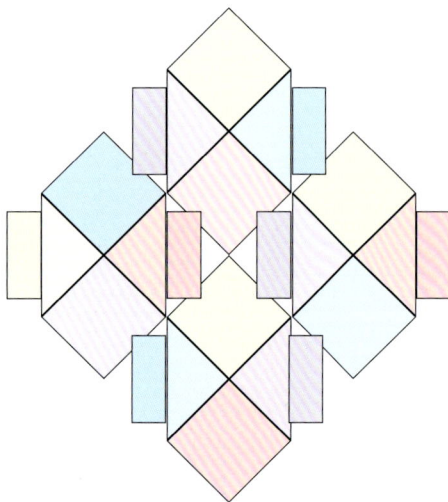

SEWING

3   Place a 2 ½" (6.5cm) square with a white 2 ½" x 4 ½" (6.5 x 11.5cm) rectangle right sides facing lining up the square to one side.

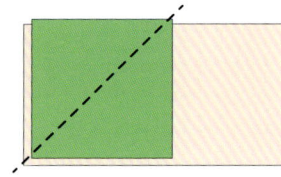

4   Sew along the drawn line. Trim the excess fabric to ¼" (0.6cm). Fold the seam to the coloured fabric and place the next 2 ½" (6.5cm) square on the opposite side. Sew it along the drawn line. Trim the excess fabric to ¼" (0.6cm).

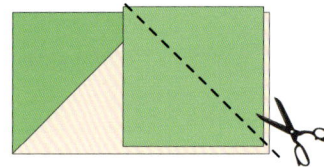

5   Press as shown by the arrows by pushing the iron towards the centre point and then on either side at the at the middle of the triangles first. This will help the piece from distorting.

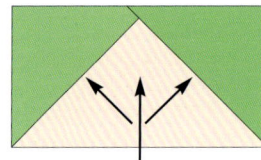

For the next steps you will need the remainder of your 2 ½" (6.5cm) squares in the same colour scheme. (Greens with greens, pinks with pinks etc).

6   Sew one to the right side of the previously sewn flying geese block.

7   Sew one on either side of the second block.

8 Then sew two 2 ½" (6.5cm) squares together with right sides facing. Sew them to the top of the previous pieces as shown.

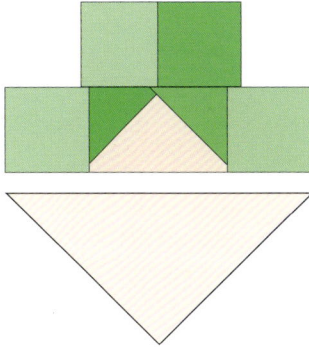

9 With the matching 6 ½" (16.5cm) half square triangle, sew it to the block.

10 Press the seam to the triangle.

11 Trim the block to 6 ¼" (16cm) square.

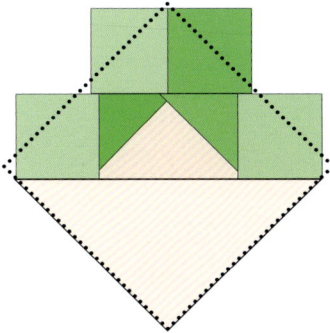

12 Lay out your blocks in a rainbow pattern alternating with low volume squares as shown.

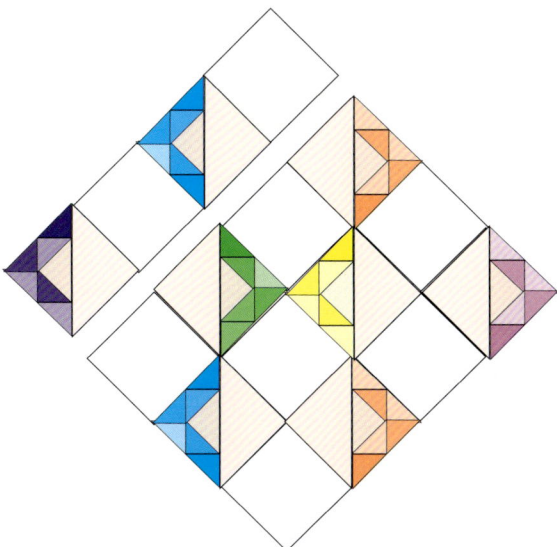

13 Sew the blocks together into rows, then the rows together.

14 Gather your dresden blades. You should have 7 purple, 7 blue, 14 green, 14 yellow, 7 orange and 7 pink.

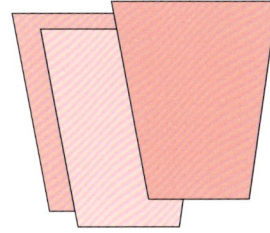

15 Reduce your stitch length on your sewing machine to 1.8.

16 Fold the first piece with right sides together lengthwise. Sew across the wide end with a ¼" (0.6cm) seam. Continue to sew the remaining pieces using chain stitching. (You do not cut the thread, and continue to sew the pieces.) When you are finished, clip them apart.

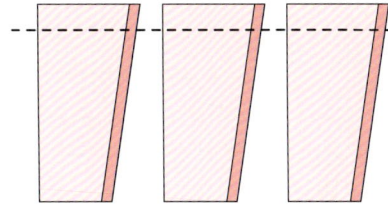

17 Using your scissors, gently turn the ends right side out to create a point. (This will make each piece look like an arrow.)

(Refer to Dresden Flower Mug Rug for turning pointers and other Dresden tips.)

18 Line up the seam directly in the centre of each blade and finger press the "point".

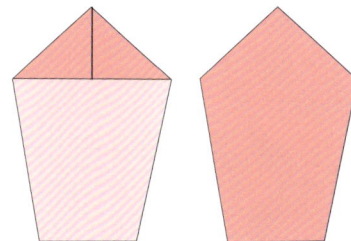

19 Place two blades together with right sides facing, lining up the points. Sew a ¼" (0.6cm) seam along the edge. Fold the seams to the left after each Dresden plate is sewn. Continue to sew on each plate in the same way.

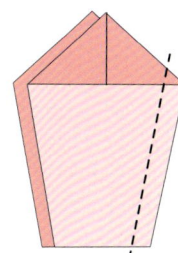

20 The first pieces will be one colour and the other half will be another colour.

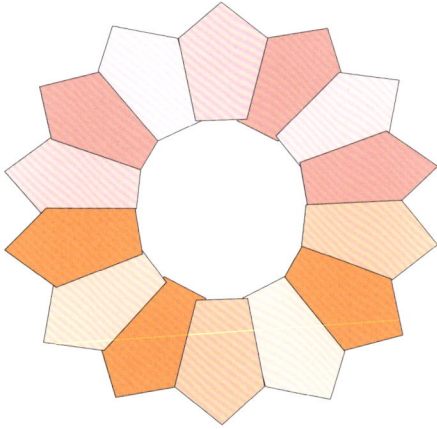

21 When you have them all sewn on, then sew the first one and last one together to make a circle.

22 Once your Dresden is sewn, turn over with right side down onto the ironing board.

Press the seams in the same direction. As you are pressing, gently pull the blades so they are flat.

23 Place the Dresden flowers onto the quilt top then take a glue stick and run the glue around the under side of the blades and then press.

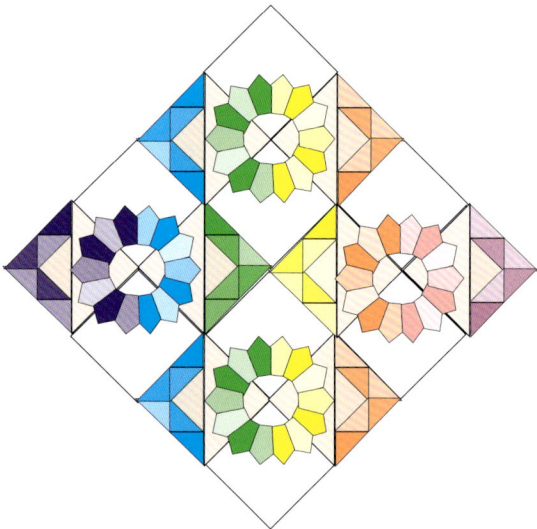

This will hold them in place while sewing. You can also pin them if you wish.

24 Layer the quilt with batting and backing.

25 Sew around each of the blades with a decorative stitch (or a straight stitch will also work).

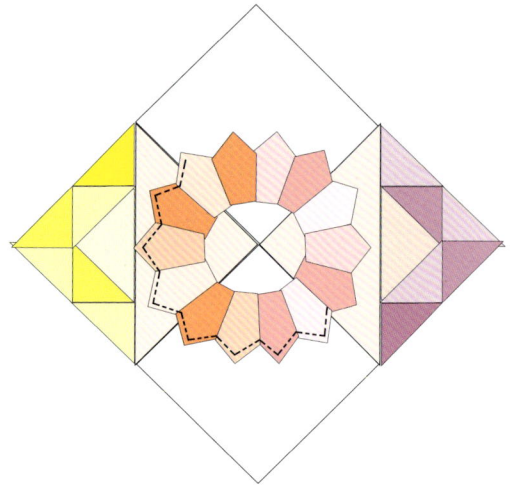

26 Fold the inner blades under and secure them with a small bit of glue.

27 Press them to keep the edges tucked under.

28 Using a decorative stitch, sew around the centre circles. Do this slowly and adjust the circle as you go to maintain its centre shape.

29 Contine to quilt the remainder of the quilt as desired.

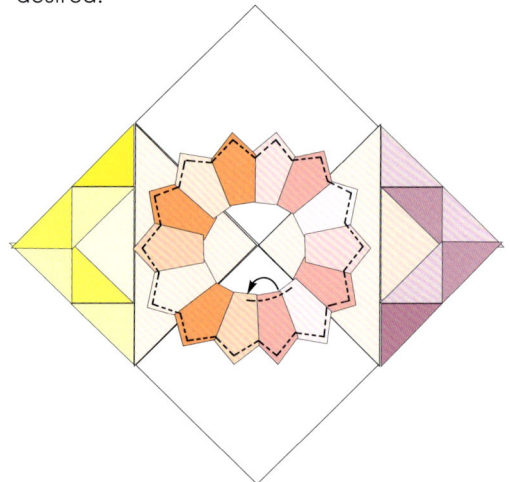

30 Sew the ends of the binding pieces together to create a long binding piece at least 90" (229cm) long.

31 Sew on the binding using the instructions on page 10.

HEXIE NEEDLEBOOK

The hunt for your English Paper Piecing supplies is over. Keep them safe and sound and eagerly awaiting your next project in this darling case. Tuck this sweet little needlebook into your Berry Busy Pack and you're all set for the upcoming retreat!

Finished Measurements
5" x 6" (13 x 15cm) Folded, 6" x 15" (15 x 38cm) Open

Materials Needed
❋ 10" (25.5cm) Square white strawberry print

❋ 10" (25.5cm) Red floral fabric

❋ 1 Pink fat quarter

❋ 5" (13cm) Square of glitter vinyl

❋ 10" (25.5cm) Square wool felt

❋ 6" x 16" (15 x 40.5cm) Heavy fusible pellon

❋ 6" x 16" (15 x 40.5cm) Thin fusible batting

❋ 1 Strawberry button

❋ 12 – ¾" (2cm) Hexie papers

❋ Matching sewing thread

❋ Parchment paper

❋ White glue

CUTTING

Using the templates cut out the following;
• 3 large hexies from the pink fat quarter, 1 needlebook inside piece and a strip 1" x 5 ½" (2.5 x 14cm)
• 3 hexies from the heavy fusible pellon
• 2 hexies from the wool felt
• 1 pocket from the glitter vinyl
• 2 hexies from the white strawberry fabric, and a strip 1" x 5 ½" (2.5 x 14cm)
• 1 – 1 ¼" (3cm) hexie and 1 needlebook inside lining piece from the thin batting

SEWING

1 Prepare your hexie by using English Paper Piecing (EPP).

2 Cut out 12 red floral pieces and 2 white strawberry pieces roughly ¼" (0.6cm) larger than the paper hexies. (Diagram 1)

3 Place the paper hexis on the wrong side of the fabric hexie and fold over the first edge. Use a quilt clip to hold it against the paper. (Diagram 2)

4 Fold the next side and using a needle and thread, stitch it in place without sewing through the paper. (Diagram 3)

5 Continue to fold down each side and stitch it to hold it in place. You do not need to knot it at the end as long as the thread holds the edge down. (Diagram 4)

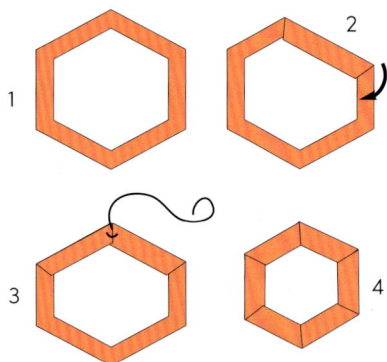

6 Press each hexie and let them cool. Remove the papers and press them again.

7 Lay a piece of parchment paper onto your ironing board. Centre each pellon hexie onto the wrong side of the three large pink hexies. Flip them over and press them for only a few seconds until they are fused to the fabric.

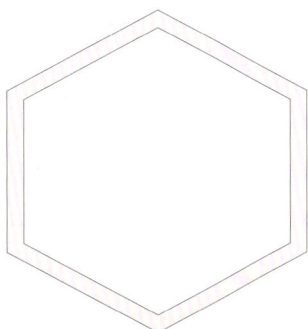

8 Place the small EPP hexies onto the right side of one large hexie creating a flower with the strawberry (white) hexie in the centre.

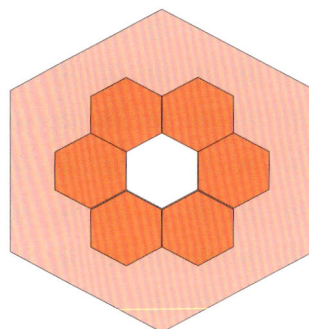

9 Once you have the desired design, put a small drop of glue on the wrong side of each hexie in the centre, and position them again. Press well with a hot iron to keep them in place.

10 Repeat this flower placement on a second large hexie (for the front and back of the needlebook).

11 Sew a decorative stitch around each hexie to hold them in place. Do the same for the second flower.

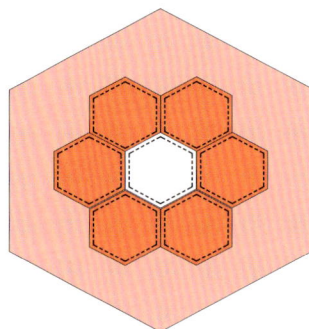

12 With both hexie flower pieces, place them right sides together, line up the heavy pellon at the corners matching them with pins. Sew them together along the pellon edge but not stitching into the pellon. Sew the remaining plain large hexie onto the right side.

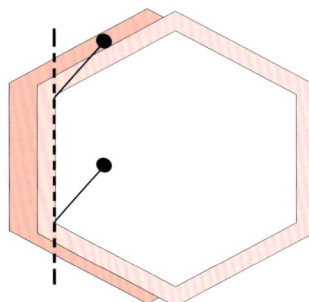

13 Using the 1" x 5 ½" (2.5 x 14cm) pink strip, fold it in half lengthwise with right sides facing. Sew it together with a ¼" (0.6cm) seam, then turn it right side out and press.

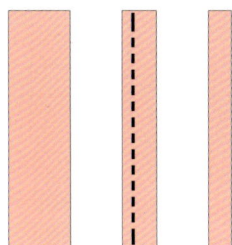

14 Place the 5 ½" (14cm) strip 1" (2.5cm) from the seam. Pin in place.

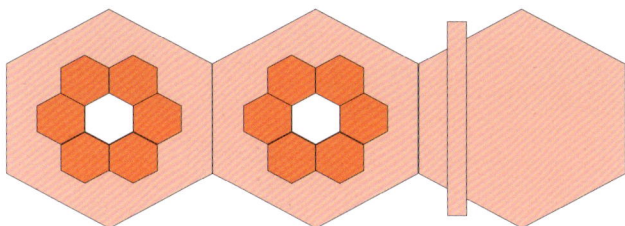

15 Gather the wool hexie, the glitter pocket, the needlebook inside piece and the inside batting piece.

16 Using the parchment on the ironing board, press the fusible batting to the wrong side of the needlebook lining.

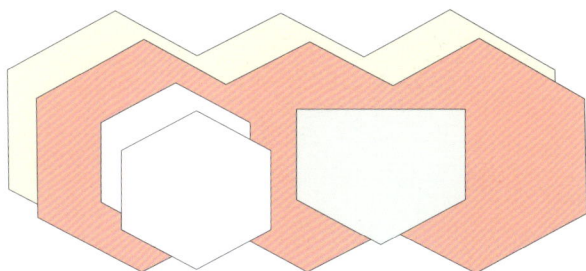

17 With the 1" x 5 ½" (2.5 x 14cm) strawberry piece, sew it to the wrong side of the glitter pocket at the top using a ¼" (0.6cm) seam. Fold it under and over to the front and topstitch it in place. Fold under the sides and the bottoms of the pocket ⅜" (1cm). You can finger press them or pin them down.

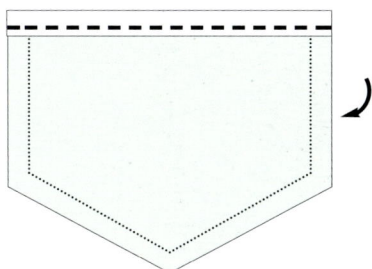

18 Using the template as a guide, line up the glitter pocket on the left side of the needlebook lining and both wool pieces on the right side. Pin in place. Sew on the glitter pocket leaving the top open and backstitching at the beginning and end.

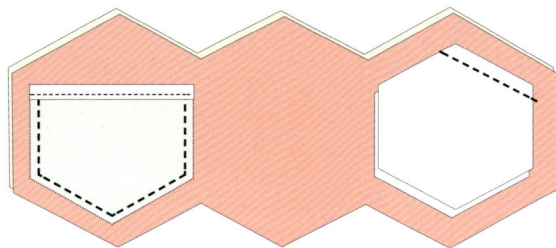

19 Sew a ¼" (0.6cm) seam along the top of the wool hexie twice to keep them in place.

20 Layer the needlebook front and back and sew around the entire shape stitching right beside the heavy pellon. Leave an opening at the right side. Trim the edges if needed, and clip all the corners. Starting from the pocket end, carefully fold it in to turn it right side out. It can be helpful to press it first and turn it while it is still warm.

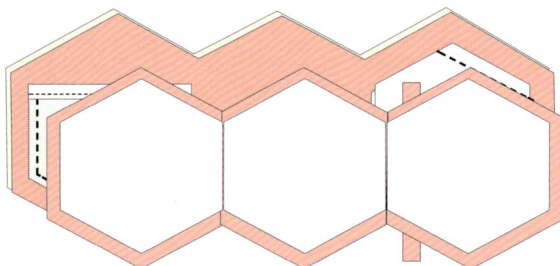

21 Gently press out the corners. Fold the opening in and whipstitch it closed. Mist the entire needlebook on the front and press well. Flip it over, cover the vinyl pocket with a piece of fabric and press.

22 Layer the strawberry hexie with right sides facing and thin batting. Sew a ¼" (0.6cm) seam leaving an opening on one side. Clip the corners. Turn it right side out and gently push out the corners. Fold the opening in and whipstitch it closed.

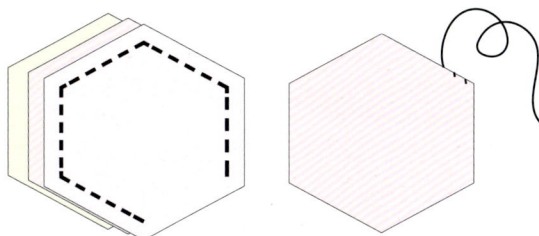

23 Place the strawberry hexie in the centre and using embroidery thread and a button, stitch it in place.

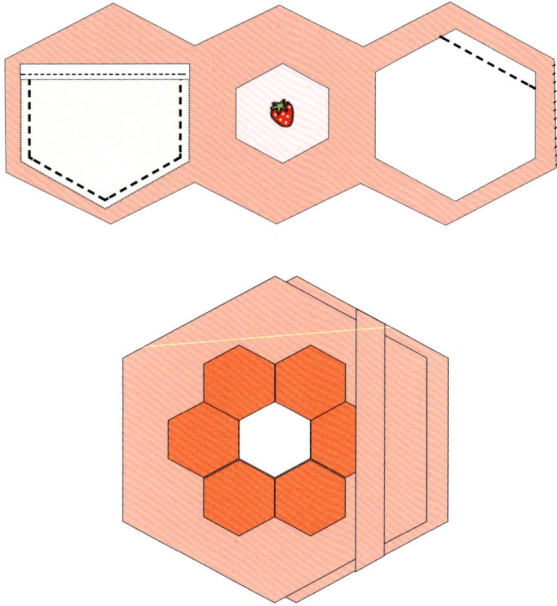

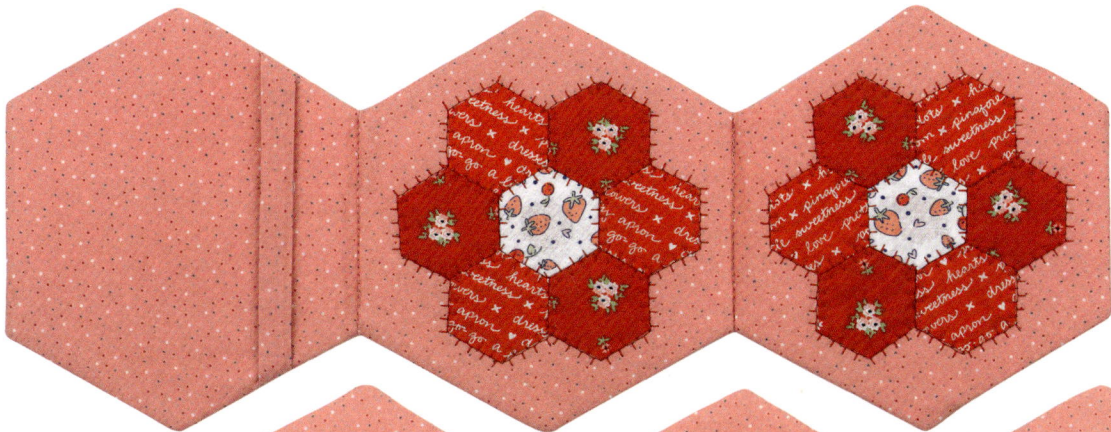

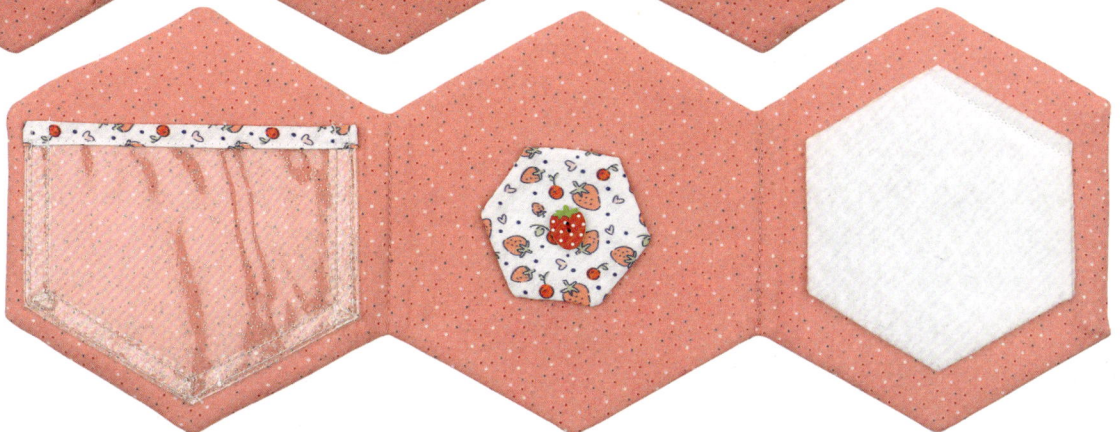

MICRO MINI STAMP QUILTS

Fabric stamps can be used for quilt tags, on pouches, or even to fix a hole in a quilt. Use them on these cute coasters to feature your most loved fabrics. Here's a handy tip – make more stamps than you need and save them for your next sewing project.

Finished Measurements
6" x 6 3/4" (15 x 17cm) – 5" x 5" (13 x 13cm) – 4" x 5" (10 x 13cm)

Materials Needed

✻ 5" (13cm) Square – 8" (20.5cm) Square depending on the desired size of the quilt

✻ 5" (13cm) Square – 8" (20.5cm) Square for backing

✻ 5" (13cm) Square – 8" (20.5cm) Square of thin fusible batting

✻ 1 ⅛" x 42" (2.8 x 107cm) Fabric strip for binding

✻ Various fabric scraps with printed images such as strawberries, bunnies, flowers or other

✻ 10" (25.5cm) Piece of low volume or white fabric

✻ 1 – 8 ½" x 11" (22 x 28cm) Sheet of Steam-A-Seam lite or Wonder Under

To make the fabric stamps;

1 Cut out your stamp fabrics with at least ¼" (0.6cm) extra fabric around the prints.

2 Pull back the first layer of the Steam-A-Seam sheet and place the fabrics wrong side down onto the sitcky side. Place the remaining fabric pieces as close together as possible.

3 Place the white or low volume fabric on the remainder of the Steam-A-Seam sheet.

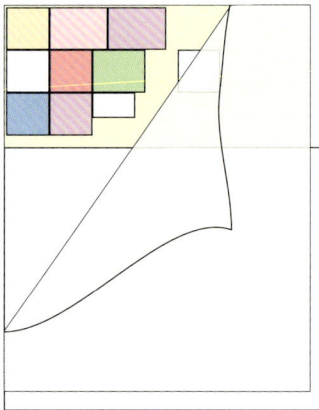

4 Place a sheet of parchment paper on top of the fabrics to protect your iron from any sticky areas that are exposed.

TIP: You may not want to use the Steam-A-Seam sheet that was pulled off because it can have some glue residue on it and make the fronts of the stamps sticky. A piece of scrap fabric or paper will also work.

5 Cut out the stamp shapes with sharp scissors. Be careful to cut them with straight lines. You can also use a dull rotary cutter blade if you wish.

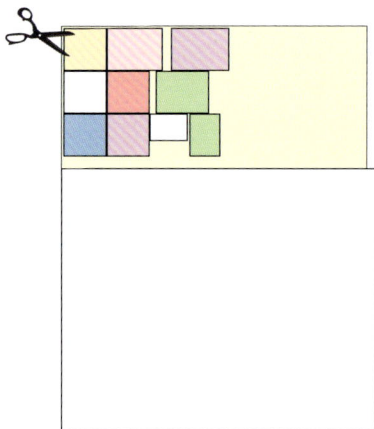

6 Remove the backing from the fabric pieces.

7 Place them onto the white or low volume fabric no closer than ⅜" – ½" (1 x 1.3cm) apart.

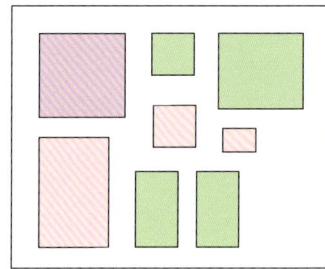

8 Cut out all of the stamps with a pair of pinking shears.

9 Carfully pull away the Steam-a-Seam from the backing of the stamps.

10 Place the stamps onto the quilt background fabric as you like.

11 Layer the top with batting and the backing.

12 Press all layers. Pin the corners if you are not using fusible batting.

13 Stitch around each stamp along the border of the inside fabric or as you desire.

For the binding, cut one- 1 ⅛" x 24" (2.8 x 61cm) - 36" (91.5cm) strip.

Please Note: The following diagrams show only the corner of the quilt. If you are able to sew a ⅛" (2.8cm) binding this is what I would recommend. DO NOT fold the binding in half lenthwise before sewing.

14 Using a ⅛" - ¼" (2.8 x 0.6cm) seam sew on the binding with the right side down, starting at the bottom front of quilt. Stop sewing when you are ⅛" - ¼" (2.8 x 0.6cm) from the corner.
(I recommend using a ⅛" (2.8cm) seam on tiny quilts.)

1/8" (0.3cm) From the edge

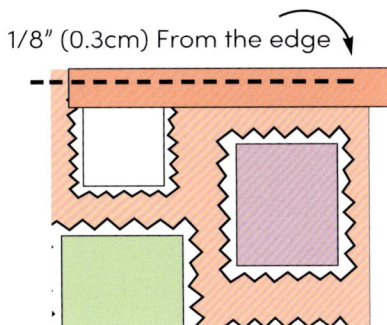

15 Lift presser foot and turn the quilt.

16 Keeping the thread attached in the machine, fold binding up as shown creating a 45° angle.

Fold Up

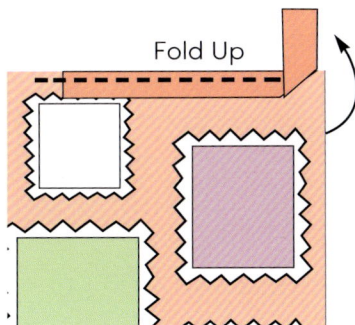

17 Fold the binding down, and continue to sew.

Fold Down

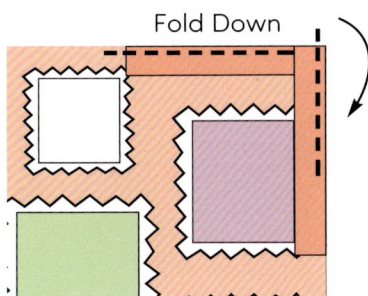

18 Repeat for all corners.

19 Fold binding to the over and under to the back and slip stich it in place. Fold corners in to create a 45° angle so they duplicate the front corners.

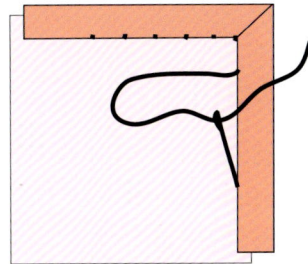

71

BERRY BUSY PACK

A small pack for travel, a perfect size for a night out with friends, or just the right size for a fun sleepover. The construction of this pack is easier than it may look, so don't be afraid to challenge yourself with this whimsical pattern.

Finished Measurements
11 ½" Tall x 9 ½" Wide x 5 ½" Deep (29 x 24 x 14cm)

Materials Needed

* ⅝ Yard (0.6m) of fabric for the backpack
* ½ Yard (0.45m) of fabric for the back inside, flap, and small pocket
* ½ Yard (0.45m) of Lining (broadcloth or thin cotton)
* 18" x 42" (45.5 x 107cm) Piece of fusible foam pellon
* Set of 2 – 1" (2.5cm) Adjustable sliders
* Set of 2 – 1" (2.5cm) Rectangular rings
* 6" (15cm) Zipper
* 14" (35.5cm) Coat or heavy zipper
* From the backback fabric; Cut two strips measuring
  3 ½" wide x 42" long (9 x 107cm)
* From the inside fabric (strawberry fabric) cut;
  1 Strip 2 ½" wide x 9" long (6.5 x 23cm)
  2 Pieces 8" x 9" (20.5 x 23cm)
* Magnetic snaps
* Matching sewing thread

CUTTING

Please Note: If you would like to make the hexie version, you will need to use the hexie instructions at the end of this pattern. Instead, you will need a piece of pellon measuring 18" x 16" (45.5 x 40.5cm) for the sides and bottom.

1 From the backpack outside fabric, the thin lining and the pellon, cut them into pieces measuring 18" x 28" (45.5 x 71cm). Sandwich the pellon in between the lining and the front fabric. Iron them to adhere them together. Stitch the layers together with criss cross stitching or any other 2 desired designs.

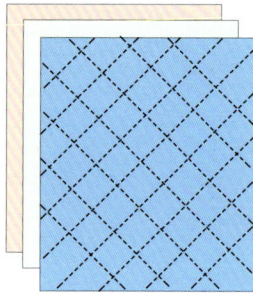

2 Cut a piece from the pellon and the flap fabric 9" x 10" (23 X 25.5cm). Layer the backpack flap fabric with the foam pellon on the wrong side and press quickly to adhere the fabric to the one side.

3 Cut the backpack back and pellon measuring 8 ½" x 10 ½" (22 X 27cm). Layer the back fabric with the foam pellon and press quickly to adhere it to the wrong side.

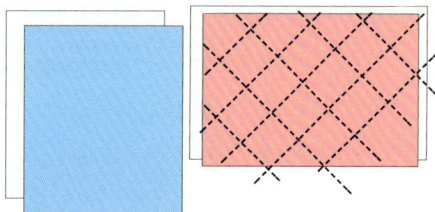

4 Cut out the templates and trace them onto the quilted pieces. Use the same templates and cut them from the inner lining fabric. Cut out all the pieces and set them aside.

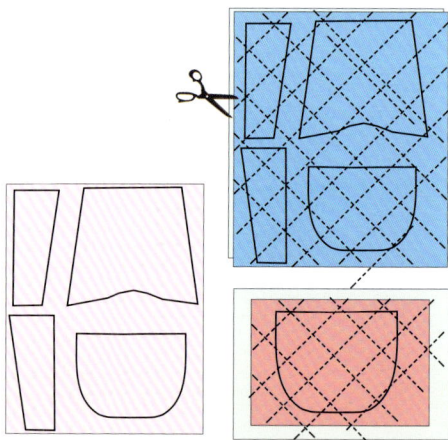

SEWING

1 With the back piece, centre the inside pocket piece right side down and 1 ½" (3.8cm) fron the top.

2 Trace the pocket zipper guide onto the wrong side of the pocket 1" (2.5cm) from the top of the inside pocket.

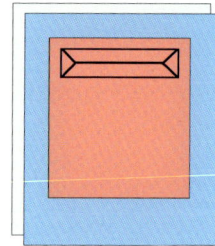

3 Sew directly on the outer rectangle line.

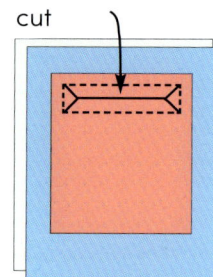

cut

4 Cut the inside lines and clip into the corners without cuting into the sewing. Turn the pocket right side to the back. Pull it firmly, but carefully leaving a very small border of the fabric showing. Press it well.

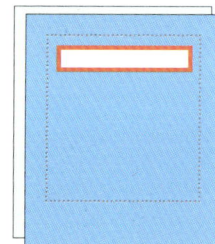

5 Open the zipper slightly and position it behind the opening and glue it in place. Press to secure it in place. (You may also use pins if you wish).

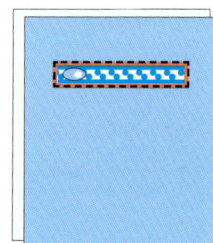

6 Sew the zipper in place. Flip it over and lay the other inside pocket piece with right sides facing and edges aligned. Pin the 2 pieces together.

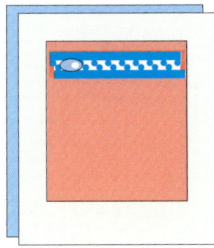

7 Bend the foam away from the pocket and sew around the entire pocket.

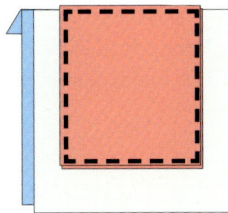

TO MAKE THE HANDLE AND STRAPS

8 Lay the foam strap piece on the ironing board and align the 39" (99cm) strip along one side. Press it quickly to hold it in place.

9 Flip it over and fold one side up and press it as you are folding it. Fold the other side over ¼" (0.6cm) and press, then fold it over the foam and press.

10 Stitch it along the edge of fold and on the opposite side. Cut off 3" (8cm) from both piecs.

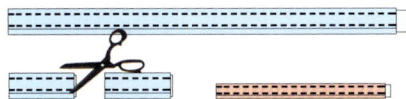

11 Do the same for the handle. You now have all the pieces to assemble the backpack.

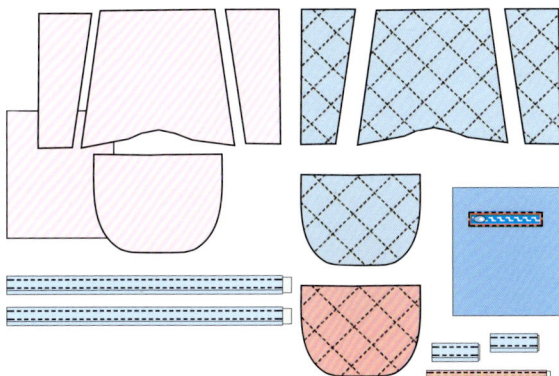

12 Fold the two 3" (8cm) strap loops in half and loop them through the 1" (2.5cm) rectangular rings. Place them along the bottom edge of the back of the backpack ¾" (2cm) from the sides. Stitch them in place.

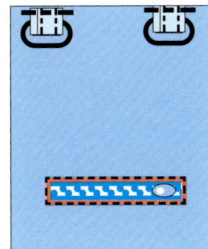

13 Line up the backpack bottom with right sides together over the loops. Sew them together with a ⅜" (1cm) seam.

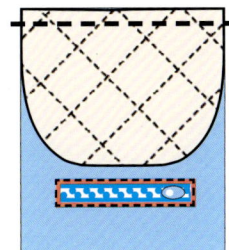

14 Topstitch ⅛" (0.3cm) from the seam.

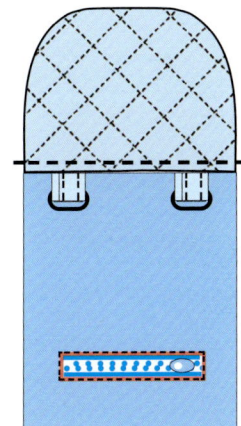

15 With right sides together sew the sides to the front with a ⅜" (1cm) seam. Topstitch ⅛" (0.3cm) from the seam.

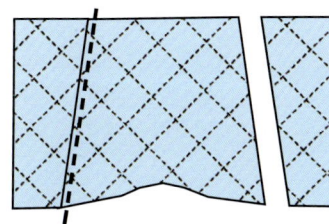

16 Mark the centres of the backpack front and back pieces by folding them in half and pinning them.

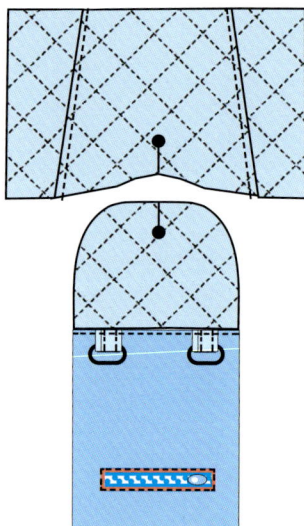

17 With right sides facing, match up the pins and begin sewing from the centre down the side. You will need to stop when you are ⅜" (1cm) from the corner.

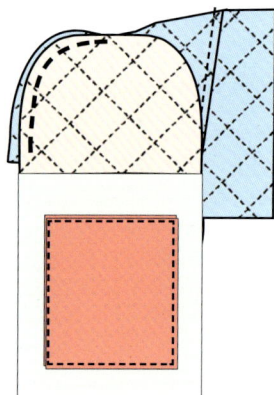

18 Do the same for the opposite side. Fold up the sides and match up the top edges, then sew either side down to the corner. Turn the bag right side out.

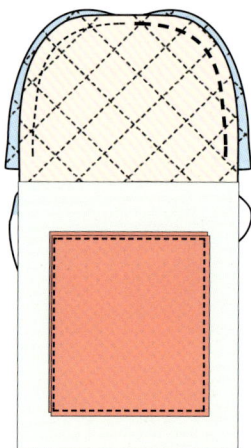

19 Position the straps 1 ¼" (3cm) from the side seams and the handle on top as shown. Pin them in place, and then sew them in place and remove the pins.

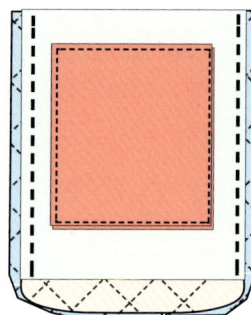

20 Place the backpack flap over the handles and centred between the side seams. Sew it in place with a ⅜" (1cm) seam.

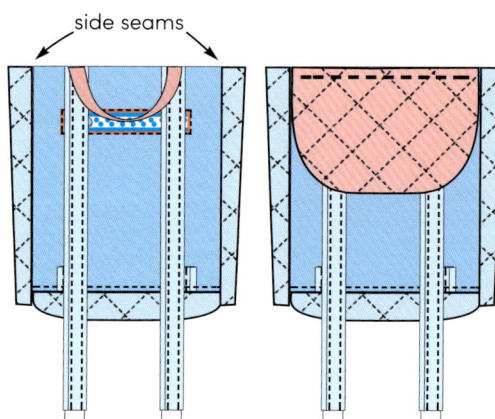

side seams

21 Open the 14" (35.5cm) zipper to the end. Fold the zipper tape down at the top stops and pin the zipper the backpack front at the left side seam.

Sew it on using a ¼" (0.6cm) seam. As you sew to the right side, allow the zipper to "pull away" the edge just before the side seam.

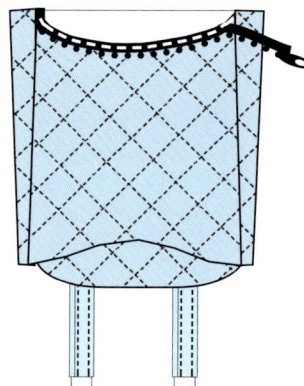

22 Sew the zipper to the opposite side in the same way. Allow the zipper to "pull away" from the sewing when you reach the side seam.

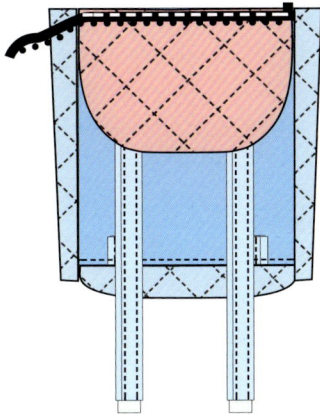

LINING

23 If you have not already done so, cut out your lining pieces.

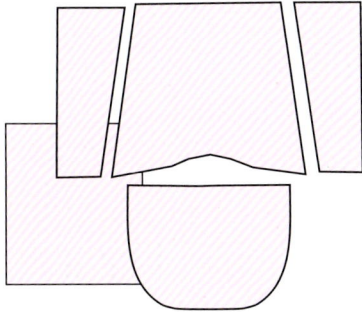

24 Sew the backpack lining with ½" (1.3cm) seams in the same way as the outer pieces were sewn. Leave one side open at least 6" (15cm) for turning. But do not turn right side out yet.

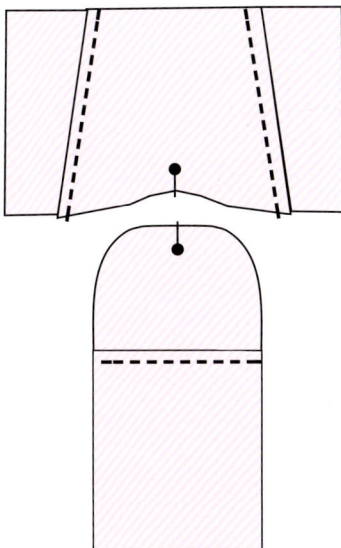

25 With right sides facing, slip the backpack into the lining matching up all of the seams. Use quilt clips or pins to hold them in place.

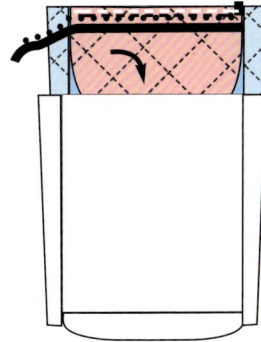

26 Stitch all the way around the bag with a ⅜" (1cm) seam. This will cover your previous zipper seams.

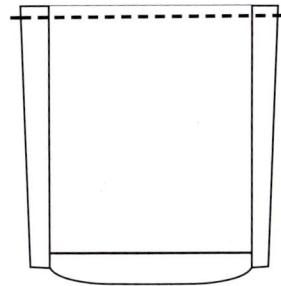

27 Turn the bag right side out and sew the opening of the lining closed.

Topstitch all the way around the top edge of the bag with a seam ½" (1.3cm) from the edge. You will need to pull the handles up to keep them out of the way.

28 Turn the bag inside out and pinch either side of the bag. Sew a 4" (10cm) seam through all the layers to create a pleat so the sides will fold in when closing.

Attach the magnetic snaps by following the manufacturers instructions onto the front flap and outside of the bag.

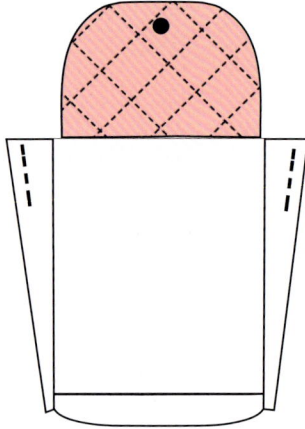

TO FINISH THE STRAPS

29 I use hardware from Emmalinebags.com and you can find instructional tutorials on their website.

30 Loop one strap through the 1" (2.5cm) adjustable slider, then loop it through the rectangular ring from the front to the back.

31 Then up into the centre of the adjustable slider, leaving about 2" (5cm). Fold the end over ½" (1.3cm) and stitch it to the strap. Do the same for the opposite strap.

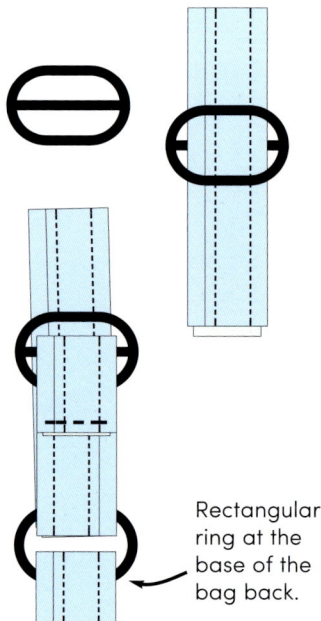

Rectangular ring at the base of the bag back.

ZIPPER END

32 Finish the end of the zipper if needed with a piece of fabric measuring 2" (5cm) square.

Sew it to the end of the zipper with both the zipper and fabric right side up. Fold the fabric up. Then fold the sides in.

Fold down and then again and hand sew it to hold it in place.

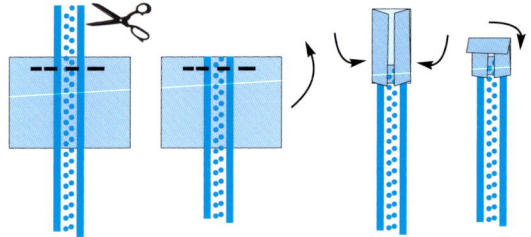

FOR THE HEXIE VERSION

1 You will need to cut approximately 20-22 hexies from the template. The more prints you use, the scrappier it will look.

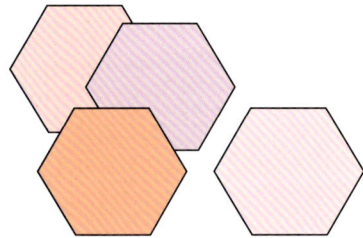

2 From the foam pellon, cut out the pack front and the flap.

Lay your hexies in the desired order to cover the flap and the pouch front pieces.

3 You will need to cut a couple of them in half to use to fill the sides.

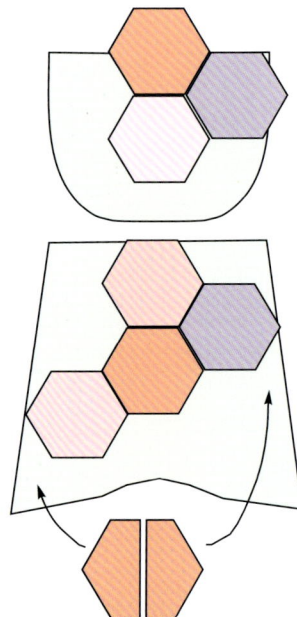

Sewing the hexies together using the sewing machine as follows;

4 **Hint:** It can be helpful to try this technique with a few hexies you will not be using on the pack to see how to create the best matching corners.

5 Sew the hexies together in columns and then sew the columns together.

Do this by placing the first two hexies together right sides facing using a ¼" (0.6cm) seam.

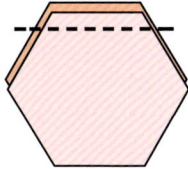

6 Once the columns are together, lay them out to be sure they are in the correct order.

7 Now sew your columns together by lining up the first edges. Sew from the edge and stop when you are ¼" (0.6cm) from the corner. (Which should be at the seam of the hexie underneath).

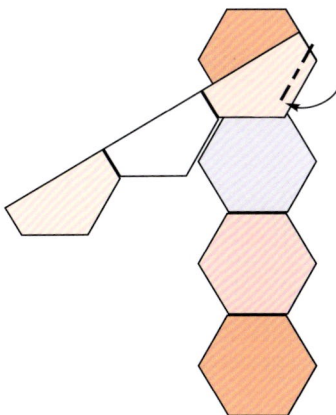

8 Lift your pressure foot and turn the pieces to line up the next side. Be sure the corner doesn't bunch by using a sylist or tool to gently lay the fabric flat. Continue to sew to the next corner right to the seam.

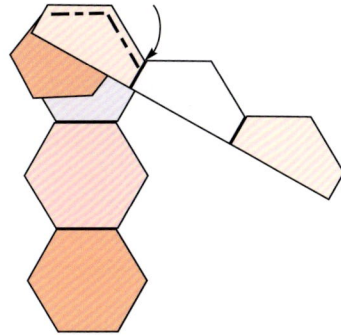

9 Keep sewing each seam in the same way, lifting the pressure foot at each corner. Once all the hexies are sewn, lay it right side down on the ironing board. Allow the corners to lay naturally and press lightly. Turn right side up and press.

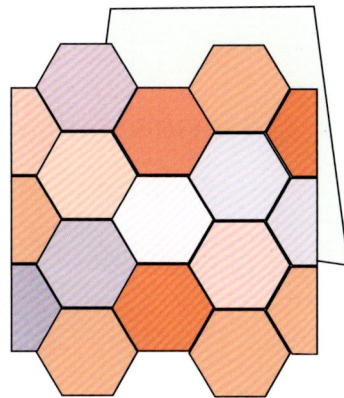

10 Lay onto the pellon and press lightly. Quilt as desired or by using the small hexie template as a guide. Do the same for the flap piece. Cut out the pieces around the pellon.

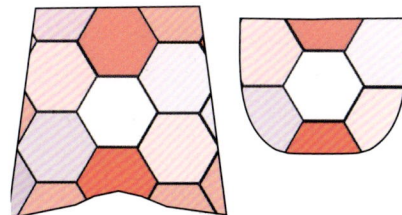

If you wish to quilt a hexie pattern onto your pieces use the template on page 116.

Continue to sew the backpack with the previous instructions on page 75.

CATHEDRAL WINDOW PILLOW

A classy new twist to the Cathedral Window block. By choosing these enchanting floral pieces or single coloured bold fabrics, you can beautifully mix up your style depending on your taste.

Finished Measurements
16" (40.5cm) Wide

Materials Needed

✳ Various fabric scraps measuring no less than
1 ½" (4cm) wide and 3 ½" (9cm) long

✳ 45" (1 ⅓ yards – 114cm) of contrasting fabric for sashing

✳ 18" x 18" (45.5 x 45.5cm) Piece of fabric for lining

✳ 18" x 18" (45.5 x 45.5cm) Piece of fabric for backing

✳ 20" (51cm) Zipper

✳ 18" – 20" (45.5 – 51cm) Pillow form

CUTTING

1 From the teal fabric cut 6 bias strips measuring 3" (8cm) wide.

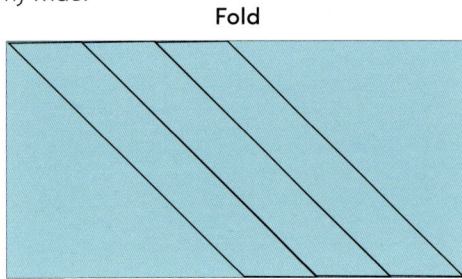

Fold

SEWING

2 Sew the scrap pieces together making 6 lengths. Two 4" (10cm) long, two 12" (30.5cm) long, and two 21" (53.5cm) long and no less than 3 ½" (9cm) wide.

3 With a glue stick, dab the glue along the entire length of the wrong side of each strip. Fold in half lengthwise and press. This will prevent the strips from stretching while sewing together.

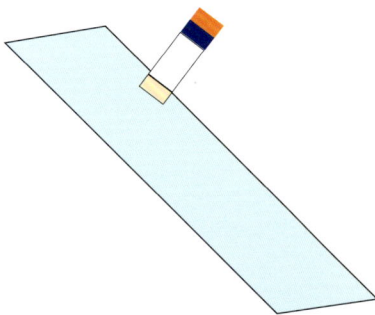

4 You will need to make 5 sections for the pillow. Two measuring 10" (25.5cm) long, two 19" (48cm) long and one 24" (61cm) long.

Do this by placing two bias strips together and sew them along the raw edges. Press the seams open.

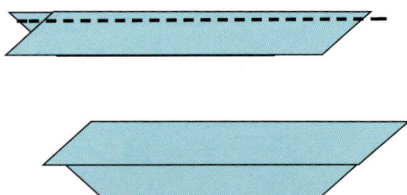

5 Lay out your lining piece to create your pillow front.

Lay on your scrappy strips as shown. Be sure to cover your corners with the shortest strips.

Lay the teal strips in between the scrappy strips. Place the long strips first and then the shorter strips.

6 Once they are in position use the gluestick and glue under each strip in the centre. Reposition the pieces as needed and then press.

Be sure the teal fabric covers the scrappy strips and overlaps them well.

7 Pin the ends down and mark on the top a 16 ½" (42cm) square. Sew around the pillow on the drawn lines. This will help to keep the edges down while sewing the Cathedral Window curves. Trim the edges.

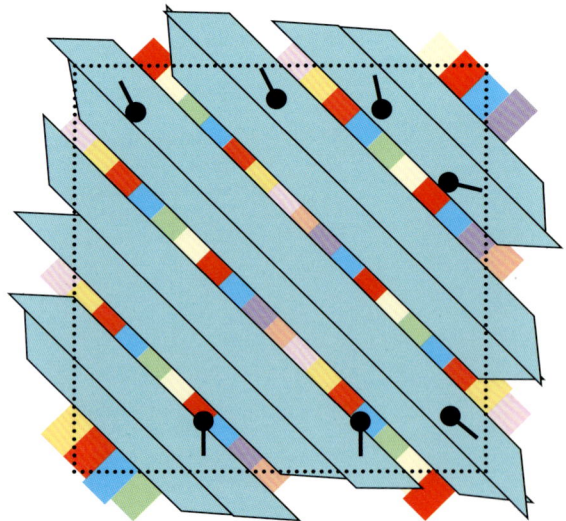

8 Using your pins, mark each spot you will be sewing to create the Cathedral Window curves.

9 Begin by marking the diagonal of the pillow. You will use this as a guide to mark the 2nd row, the 4th row, the 7th row and the 9th row.

10 Measure each row with a dress maker's measuring tape and fold it evenly into 3, into 4 and into 5 for the remainder of the rows. Mark each spot with a pin. Each pin will be approximately 4" (10cm) apart.

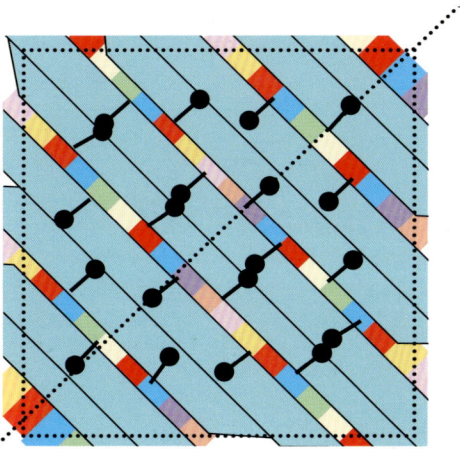

11 Using matching thread and fold each section between the pins down. Topstitch along the edge. Sew at a slow and even pace to be sure the folds do not bunch up.

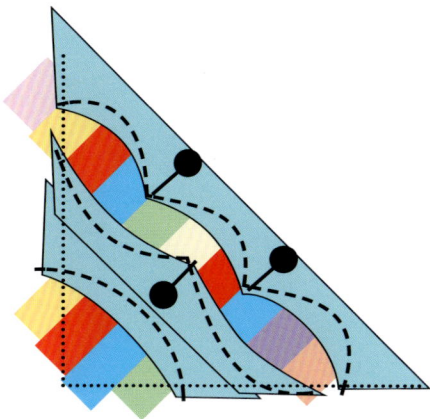

12 Continue to sew each section down.

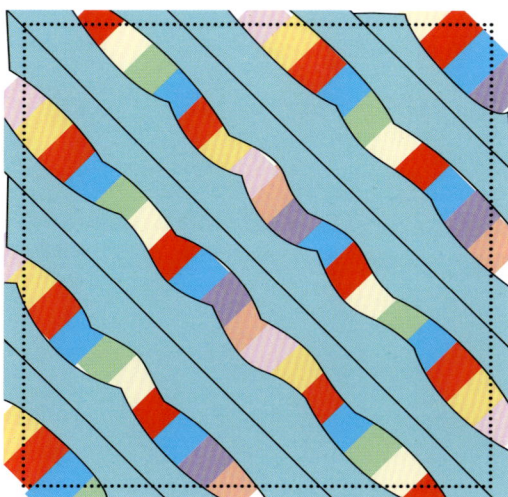

13 To sew on the zipper, use the backing fat quarter and lay it right side up and zipper right side down along the salvage edge. You may need to place it about 1" (2.5cm) from the edge so that the sewing covers the salvage. This is used so that you do not need to finish this edge.

Sew the zipper on along the zipper tape.

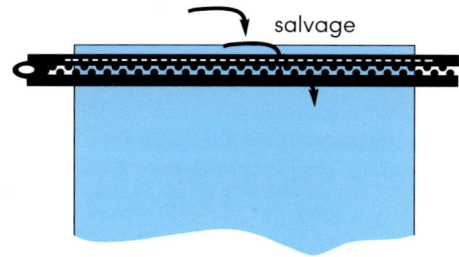

salvage

14 Now fold the fabric to cover the zipper teeth and half of the zipper tape. This will make a "lip" to hide the zipper.

Pin in place and then press. Sew a seam along the layers through the zipper tape to hold it in place.

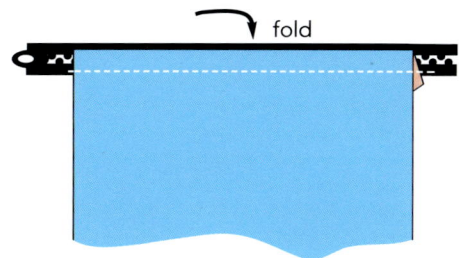

fold

15 Open the zipper about 5" (13cm). Place the pillow front and back together with right sides facing. Sew slightly inside the 16 ½" (42cm) markings previously sewn around the edges of the pillow.

Be careful to keep the lip of the zipper covering out of the way while sewing. Trim edges. Turn right side out and press.

pull down and pin if needed

LAP QUILT

Colourful waves turn a classic block into a quilt with movement to delight the eye. This beginner friendly design is a playful beauty that can be from your fat quarter collection.

Finished Measurements
50" x 72" (127 x 183cm)

Materials Needed

✳ 6 Teal fat quarters 18" x 22" (45.5 x 56cm)

✳ 6 Purple fat quarters

✳ 9 pieces of low volume fabric 8" x 42" (20.5 x 107cm) strips

✳ Matching sewing thread

✳ Cut the teal and purple fat quarters into
2 ½" (6.5cm) strips 18" (45.5cm) long

✳ Cut the low volume fabric into one 2 ½" (6.5cm) strip and
one 4 ½" (11.5cm) strip

✳ 55" x 80" (140 x 203cm) Piece of batting

CUTTING

Prepare your purple strips by cutting them into 8 of each. Begin cutting the longer strips then the shorter strips.

18 ½" (47cm) strips

16 ½" (42cm)

12 ½" (32cm)

8 ½" (22cm)

6 ½" (16.5cm)

2 ½" (6.5cm)

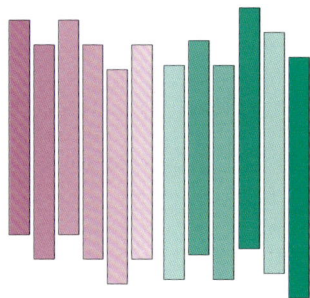

Cut your teal strips into 8 of each. Begin by cutting the longer pieces first.

18½" (47cm)

14½" (37cm)

12½" (32cm)

10½" (27cm)

6½" (16.5cm)

4½" (11.5cm)

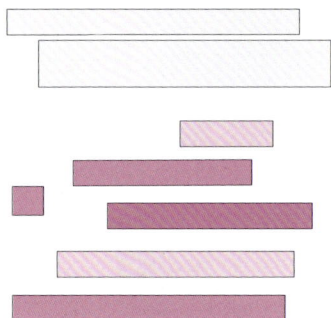

Please Note: The low volume fabric is cut as you sew to ensure proper lengths.

SEWING

1 Sew your purple blocks first beginning with the 2 ½" (6.5cm) squares. Place them right side down on randomly chosen 2 ½" (6.5cm) strips cut from the low volume fabric.

2 Chain piece them together as shown. Press the seams towards the purple fabric.

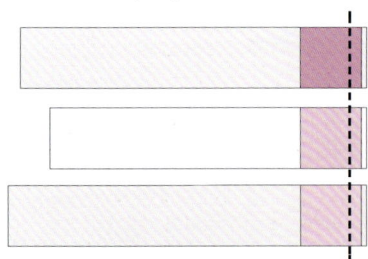

3 Cut off the low volume fabric so that your piece now measures 6 ½" (16.5cm) long. Sew the 6 ½" (16.5cm) purple strips to the blocks. Press the seam towards the purple fabric.

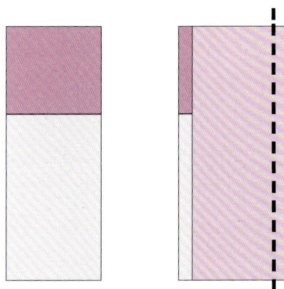

4 Chain piece your next low volume 2 ½" (6.5cm) strip with right sides facing. Cut the blocks apart using the edge of the block as a guide. (As shown by the dotted lines.)

5 Press the seam towards the low volume strip.

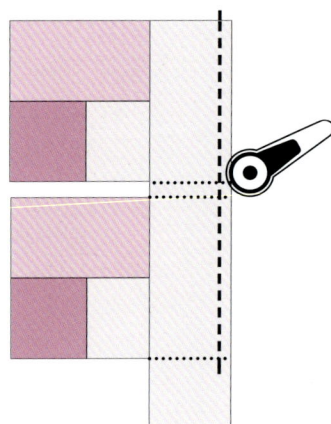

6 Sew on the 8 ½" (22cm) pieces right sides facing. Press the seams towards the purple fabric.

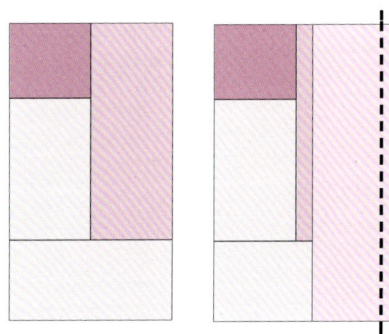

7 Chain piece a 4 ½" (11.5cm) strip next and press seams towards the low volume fabric. Cut the blocks apart using the edge of the block as a guide. (Along the dotted lines.)

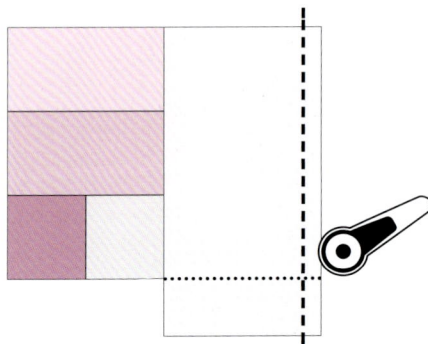

8 Sew on the 12 ½" (32cm) pieces right sides facing. Press the seams towards the purple fabric.

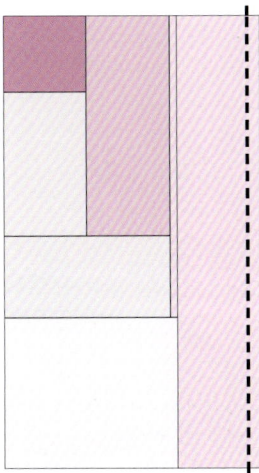

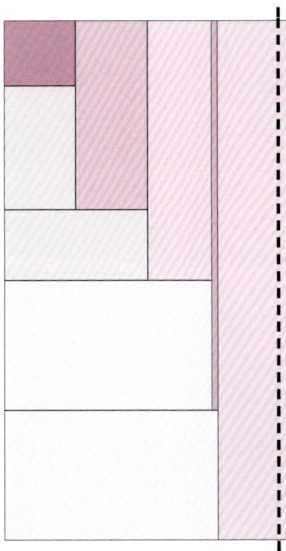

9 Chain piece your next low volume 4 ½" (11.5cm) strip with right sides facing. Cut the blocks apart using the edge of the block as a guide. (As shown by the dotted lines.) Press the seam towards the low volume strip.

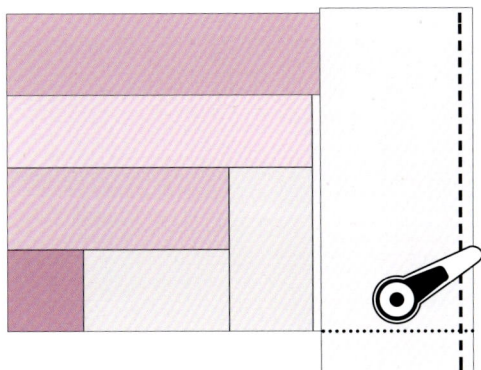

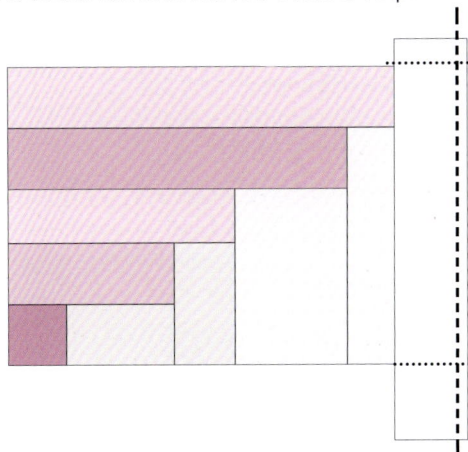

10 Sew on the 16 ½" (42cm) pieces right sides facing. Press the seams towards the purple fabric.

11 Chain piece your next low volume 2 ½" (6.5cm) strip with right sides facing. Cut the blocks apart using the edge of the block as a guide. (As shown by the dotted lines.)

Press the seam towards the low volume strip.

12 Sew on the 18 ½" (47cm) pieces right sides facing. Press the seams towards the purple fabric.

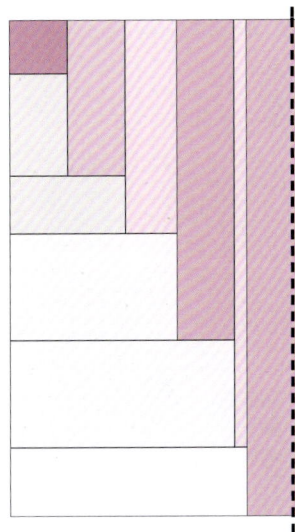

13 The finished purple block.

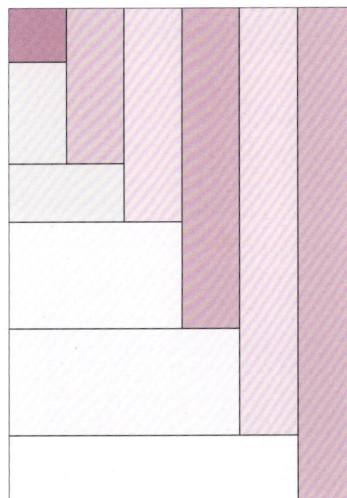

14 The teal blocks are sewn in the same way, just a slightly different order. Begin with the 4 ½" (11.5cm) teal piece. Chain piece a 2 ½" (6.5cm) low volume strip to each end.

15 Press seams towards the teal fabric. Trim off the strip so the piece measures 6 ½" (16.5cm). Sew on the 6 ½" (16.5cm) piece. Press seams towards the teal fabric. Chain piece on a 4 ½" (11.5cm) strip.

16 The low volume fabric strips are now pressed towards the teal fabric instead of towards the low volume fabric like the purple blocks.

17 Follow the diagram as shown. 10 ½" piece

2 ½" (6.5cm) low volume strip – cut the blocks apart. 12 ½" (32cm) piece

2 ½" (6.5cm) low volume strip – cut the blocks apart.

14 ½" (37cm) piece

4 ½" (11.5cm) low volume strip – cut the blocks apart.

Press well.

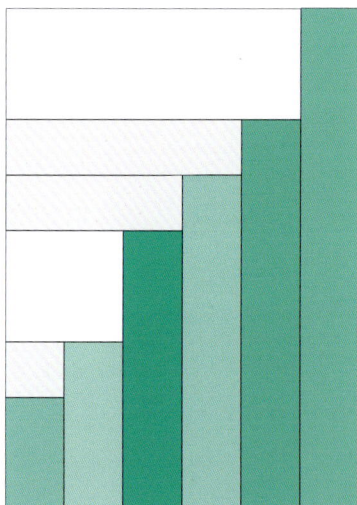

18 The diagram on the right side shows the placement for the quilt, but there are many variations you can make.

Move around the blocks until you have your desired design.

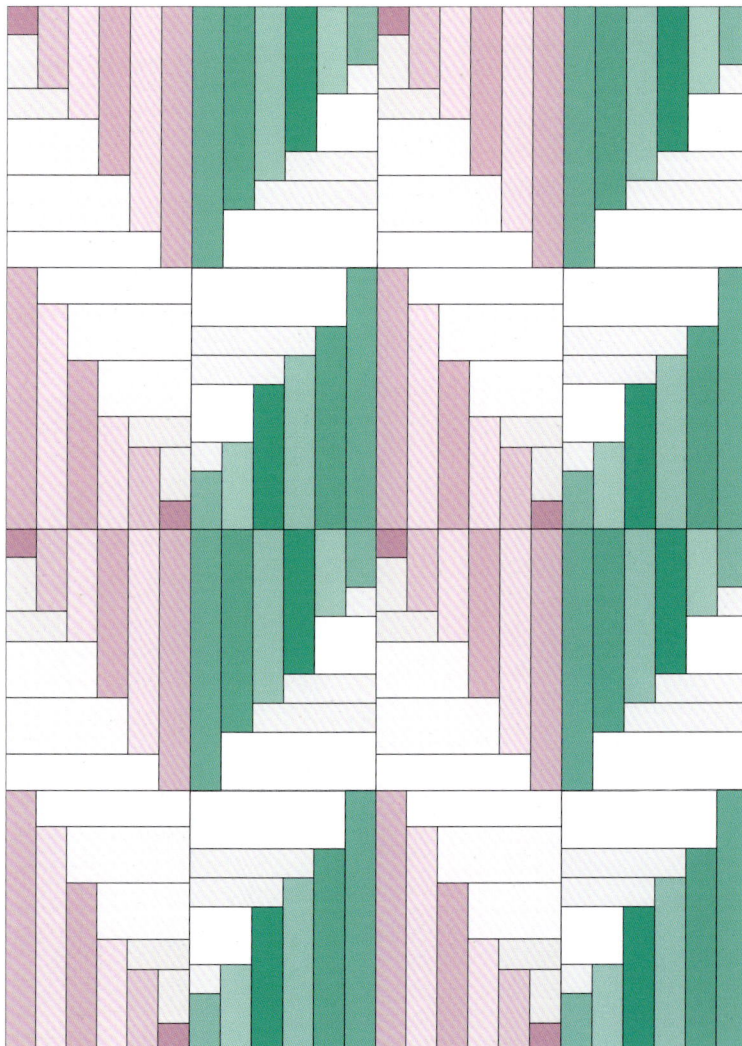

LOG CABIN MINI

Log Cabin blocks sewn together to make a Sawtooth Star are the perfect combination for this delicate mini quilt. Showcase it amongst your mini quilts or set it out as a table centrepiece for everyone to enjoy.

Finished Measurements
10 ½" x 10 ½" (27 x 27cm)

Materials Needed

✳ Purple and low volume various scraps measuring no less than 1" x 3 ½" (2.5 x 9cm) long

✳ 8 Low volume fabric squares 3 ½" x 3 ½" (9 x 9cm)

✳ 13" x 13" (33 x 33cm) piece of fabric for backing

✳ 13" x 13" (33 x 33cm) piece of thin batting

✳ 1 – 3" x 42" (8 x 107cm) Strip cut into 2 – 1 ½" (3.8cm) strips for binding

✳ 12" x 12" (30.5 x 30.5cm) Piece of batting

✳ Matching sewing thread

BASIC PAPER PIECING INSTRUCTIONS

STEP 1: Fold the template on the stitching line between pieces a and b (Figure 1). Unfold the template.

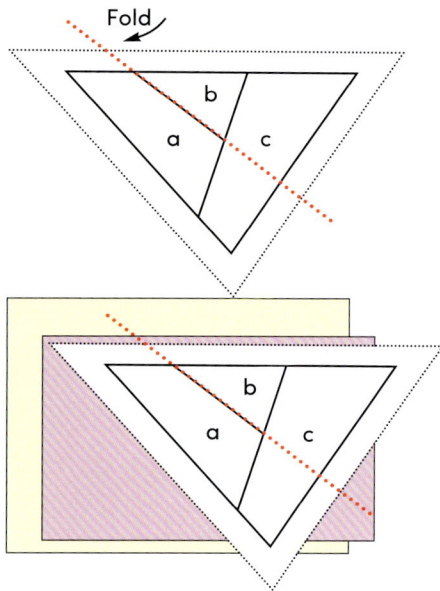

Figure 1

STEP 2: Using a piece of fabric large enough to cover piece a and the seam allowance around it, place the reverse side of the fabric to the back of the foundation template. Using a piece of fabric large enough to cover piece b, place it right sides together with fabric covering piece a (Figure 2).

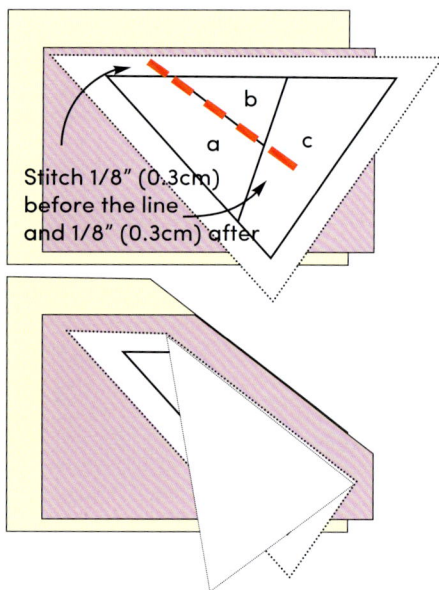

Figure 2

To ensure that your piece b fabric is in the correct position, align it while the template is folded. At the least, it should cover the area when folded.

STEP 3: Carefully pick up the fabric and template set and move to your machine. Unfold the template and stitch the line between a and b. Start sewing ⅛" (0.3cm) before the line and stitch ⅛" (0.3cm) beyond the line.

STEP 4: With the template folded on the line, trim the seam allowance ⅛" (0.3cm) to ⅜" (1cm) from the folded edge of the template.

STEP 5: Fold fabric the seam and finger press.

STEP 6: Repeat steps 1 through 6 for each numbered piece working sequentially (e.g. a/b, b/c, c/d).

STEP 7: Gently tear away foundation from the extra stitching in piece c to the line between pieces b and c.

STEP 8: Repeat steps 1 through 7 for each letatered piece working sequentially (e.g. a/b, b/c, c/d).

STEP 9: Once the piece is completed, trim to the seam allowance.

Repeat for each template.

JOINING THE TEMPLATE PIECES

Using your desired pattern, sew all of your template pieces using the Basic Paper Piecing Instructions listed on page 8.

With right sides together, place a straight pin through the points on the corners on both ends. Use pins or fabric clips along the seam as necessary. If the seam alignment is critical, baste those areas to ensure that your seams align before your final stitching. After joining two template pieces, ensure that they are properly aligned.

Remove the paper from the seam allowance only before adding the next template piece. Complete each block or panel for your pattern.

Join the blocks or panels using the pattern as a guide. Use pins or fabric clips to match critical seam alignments. If your foundation paper is making it difficult to match seams for these panels, remove the paper backing being careful to not stretch the fabric. Otherwise, remove the paper backing after all piecing has been completed.

GENERAL PAPER PIECING TIPS

Align a piece of cardstock on the line you intend to fold. Fold to the cardstock. Remove the cardstock and crease your fold.

Always overestimate the size of fabric you'll need for each piece PLUS the seam allowances.

Select a thread that blends with most of your fabrics.

Use an open-front presser foot which allows you to clearly see your stitching. Set your stitch length to 14 to 18 stitches per inch.

Mistakes can happen! Keep a seam ripper handy.

TINY TIPS

If you're having difficulty catching the fabric on the feed dogs as you slide it in place to stitch, slip a scrap of paper under the unit being sewn before sliding it under the needle. Tear away the scrap paper after stitching.

Trim thread tails after each seam.

Finger pressing will be sufficient for these tiny pieces, but if you do need to press, use a hot, dry iron.

After joining pieces and panels, trim seam allowances that extend beyond the pattern template. Have tweezers handy to remove small pieces of paper.

SEWING

1 Print and cut out 8 paper pieced templates from page 119. Using various purple and pink fabrics, follow the paper piecing instructions and make all 8 log cabin blocks.

2 Press the blocks and remove the papers. Cut 4 of the blocks in half diagonally to make 8 triangles.

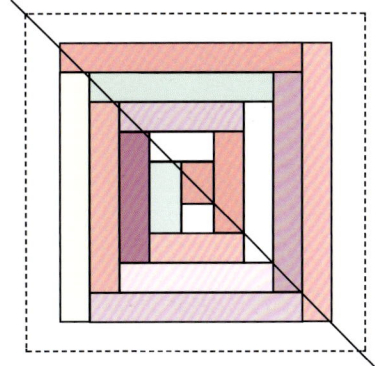

3 From the template to the on page 120, cut 8 pieces from random low volume fabrics.

4 Sew a log cabin triangle to the low volume pieces. Press the seam towards the low volume piece.

From the low volume fabrics cut 4 squares 3" (8cm) squares. Piece the blocks together to create a star pattern as shown. Sew the pieces together in rows, and then sew the rows together.

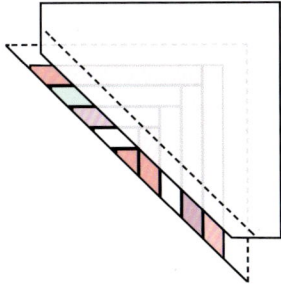

5 Layer the quilt with thin batting and backing. Press all the layers together. You may wish to sew a tiny seam around the entire outside edge to keep the layers together. Use a big basting stitch very close to the edge. Trim the quilt around all edges.

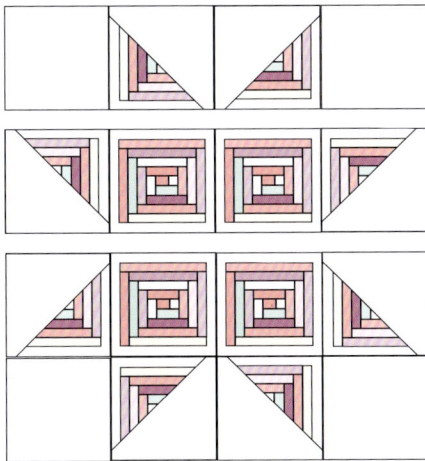

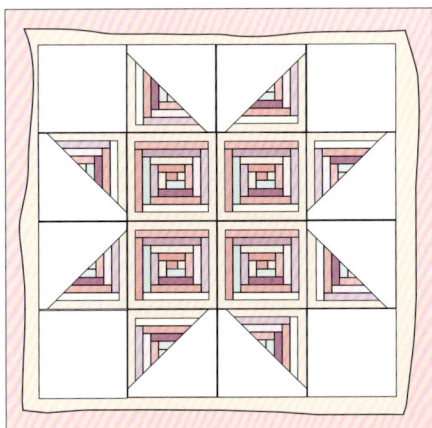

6 Layer the quilt with thin batting and backing. Press all the layers together. You may wish to sew a tiny seam around the entire outside edge to keep the layers together. Use a big basting stitch very close to the edge. Trim the quilt around all edges.

BINDING INSTRUCTIONS

Please Note: The following diagrams are only showing one block, but it is to show the corner of the quilt.

1 For the binding, cut one – 1 ½" (3.8cm) strip.

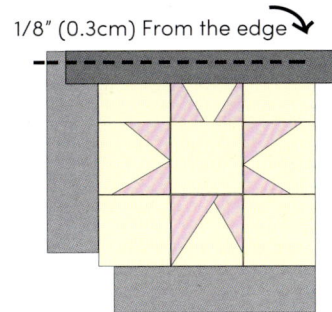

1/8" (0.3cm) From the edge

2 Using a ⅛" (0.3cm) seam, sew on the binding with the right side down, starting at the bottom of the mini quilt. Stop sewing when you are ⅛" (0.3cm) from the corner. Lift presser foot and turn the quilt.

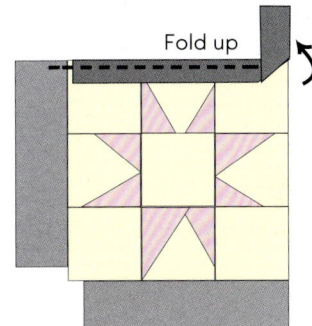

Fold up

3 Keeping the thread attached in the machine, fold binding up as shown.

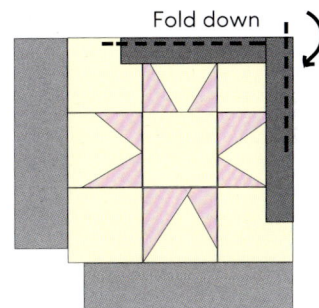

Fold down

4 Now fold the binding down, and continue to sew a ⅛" (0.3cm) seam along the border. Repeat for all corners.

5 Fold binding to the back and handstitch with small slip stitches. Fold corners in to create a 45° angle so they duplicate the front corners.

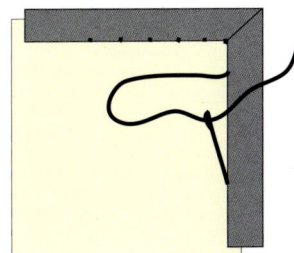

POUCH PURSE

Perfect for makeup or sewing supplies, this fully lined pouch quickly turns into a purse by simply adding a strap to the side loops. Use your treasured fabric pieces, or skip the scrappy look and use your favourite fabric for an afternoon project sure to please.

Finished Measurements
8 ¼" Tall x 8 ½" Wide (21 x 22cm)

Materials Needed

✳ Various pieces of fabric to cover the pouch front

✳ 18" x 22" (45.5 x 56cm) Piece of foam pellon or heavy batting

✳ 1 Fat quarter for the lining

✳ 18" (45.5cm) Zipper

For the straps;

✳ Various pieces of fabric to make a strap 3" x 55" (8 x 140cm) long

✳ Pellon 1 ¼" wide x 55" long (3 x 140cm)

✳ 2 Lobster claw hooks

✳ Matching sewing thread

SEWING

1 Cut out the template on page 120 and trace it onto one side of the foam pellon or heavy batting. (A Sharpie works well for this).

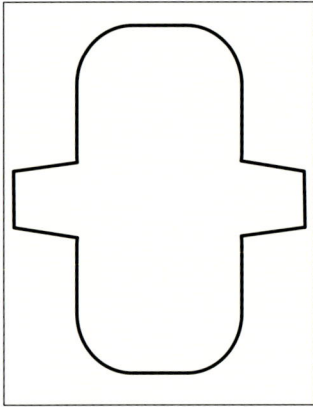

2 Place your scraps on top of the pellon in a patchwork manor. Once you have a few pieces, begin to sew them together.

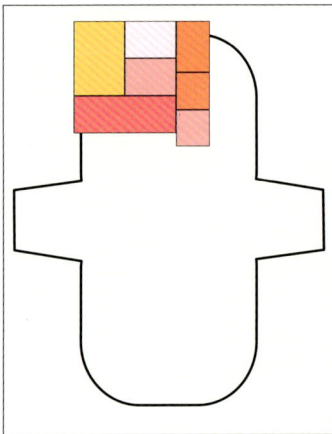

3 Continue to add more pieces until the patchwork covers the entire pouch shape.

You may need to sew a few pieces together first and then add them to the main patchwork pieces. You can also trim the pieces down to fit nicely together.

4 Once you have covered the template area, you can sew the pieces to the pellon by quilting them on.

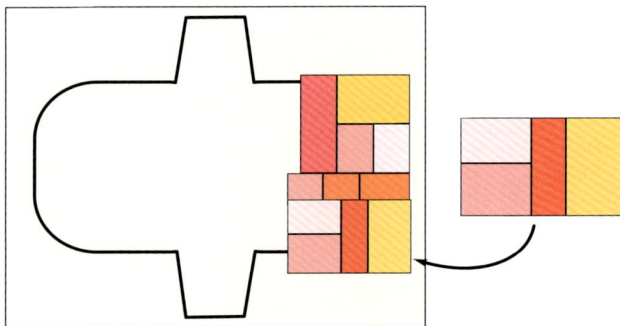

5 Draw the template onto the patchwork pieces and cut out the template shape.

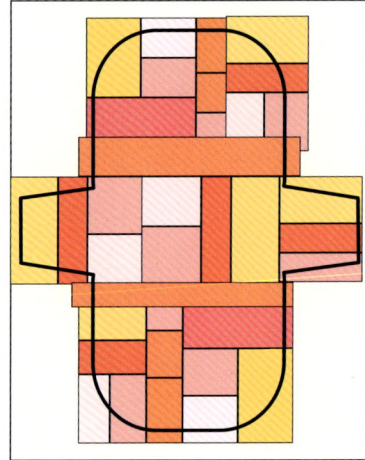

6 Sew two patchwork strips measuring at least 1 ¾" wide x 16 ½" (4.5 x 42cm) long.

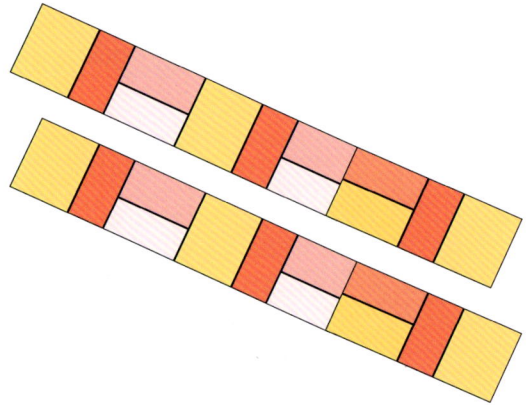

7 Trim the strip to 1 ¾" (4.5cm) wide.

8 Place the 22" (56cm) zipper in between the patchwork strip and the 2" x 16 ½" (5 x 42cm) lining strip. Sew through all the layers as close to the zipper teeth as possible.

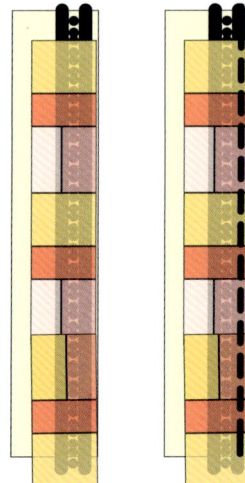

9 Place a pellon strip on top of the seam, just along the stitching for the zipper.

10 Sew it on directly beside the previous stitching. This reduces the bulk of the pellon right along the zipper. Fold the fabric over the pellon and press.

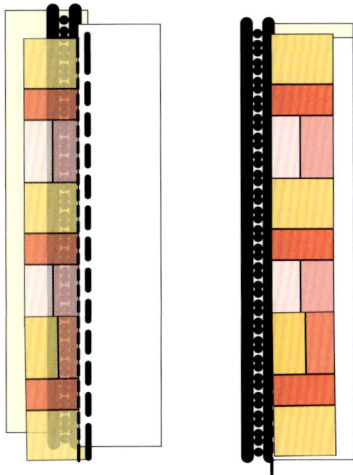

11 Do the same to the other side of the zipper repeating the last three steps.

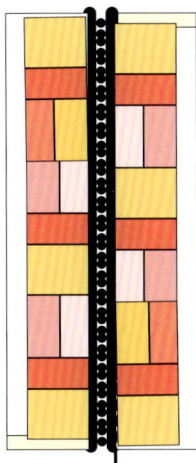

12 Topstitch along the zipper ¼ (0.6cm) from the zipper teeth. Trim each side 1 ½" (3.8cm) from the zipper.

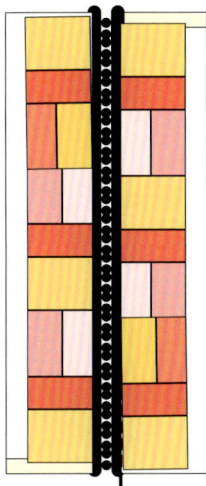

13 Cut a piece of fabric for the pouch loops that measures 2 ½" x 6" (6.5 x 15cm). Fold it right sides together and sew along the 6" (15cm) side.

14 Turn right side out. Cut in half to make two pieces for the pouch side loops. Press.

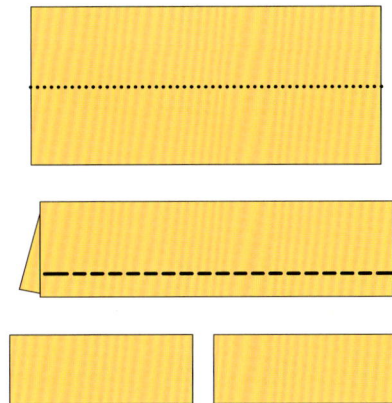

15 Fold the loop in half and pin in place at the bag side.

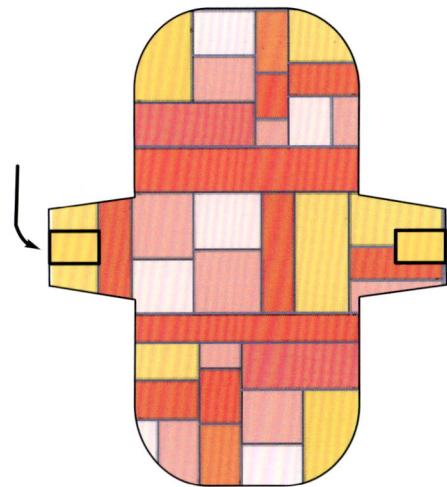

16 Place the zipper right side down covering the loop. Sew across the end. Do the same to the opposite side of the pouch.

17 Mark each side of the pouch at the centre top and at the middle of the zipper section.

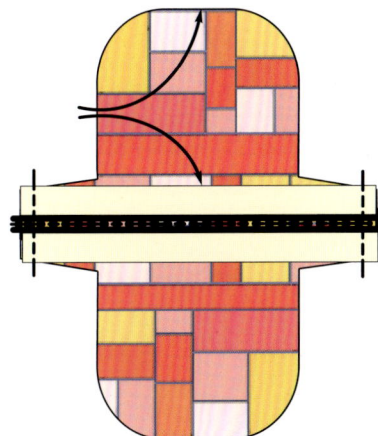

18 Match up the markings and using quilt clips, secure the zipper piece to the pouch side.

19 Sew it in place starting at the centre marking, down to the side, then from the marking to the other side.

Repeat for the opposite side of the pouch.

LINING

20 Cut a 6" (15cm) slit into the middle of the pouch lining as shown. Fold over the sides of the pouch ¼" (0.6cm) and press. Sew the sides to the pouch fronts.

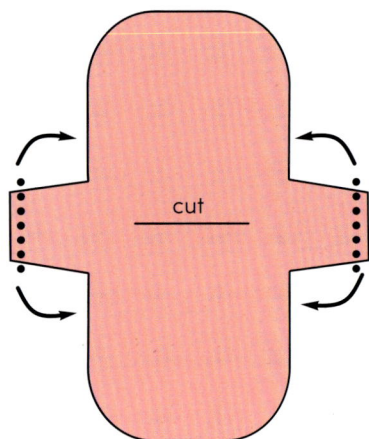

cut

Your lining will look like this.

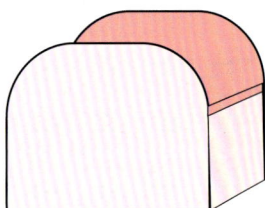

21 Insert the pouch into the lining. One side facing you (side 1) and the other side facing away from you (side 2).

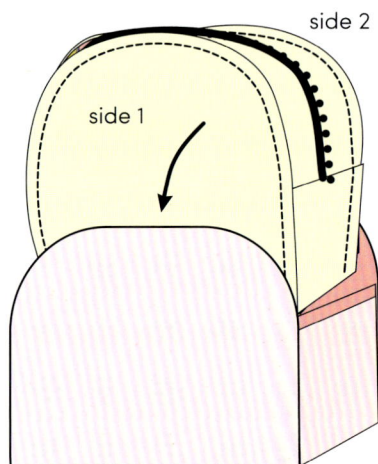

side 2

side 1

22 Squish side 1 of the pouch down and line up the lining to side 2. Use quilt clips or pins to hold it in place.

23 Sew a ¼" (0.6cm) seam along the top from the pouch side to the opposite side to the point where the fabric is folded over.

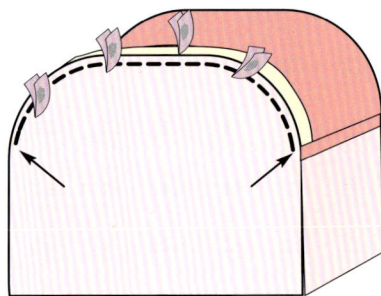

24 Turn the lining right side out and then do the same to the lining on the opposite side.

25 Turn the lining right side out. Handstitch the sides and the opening at the bottom of the pouch.

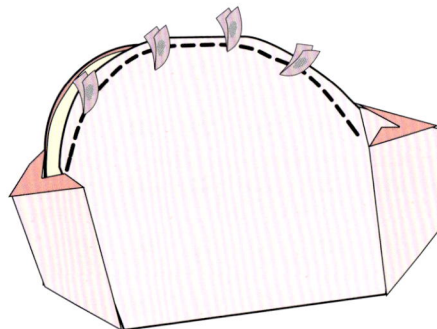

26 Turn the pouch right side out and fold a piece of batting to fill the pouch generously. Using the batting to keep the pouch firm, press the pouch and all the seams. Remove the batting.

27 If you would like a handle or strap, sew one in the same way as the busy pack to the length you need. Add lobster claw hooks to either end and hook onto the loops at the sides of the pouch.

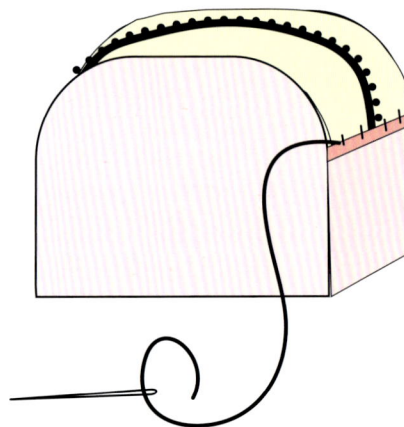

DIAMOND PINCUSHION

Diamonds are a girl's best friend, and definitely shine on this handy pincushion. Use the secret pocket on the bottom to keep your scissors safe, and the side pockets to keep your sewing supplies accessible.

Finished Measurements
2" (5cm) Tall, 6 ½" (16.5cm) Long, 2 ½" (6.5cm) Wide

Materials Needed

✱ 3 - 2 ½" (6.5cm) Squares of an assortment of colours

✱ 8 - 2 ½" (6.5cm) Squares of low volume prints

✱ 2 ½" x 7" (6.5 x 18cm) Piece of blue fabric

✱ 2" (5cm) Strip of blue fabric

✱ 3" (8cm) Strip of low volume fabric for base

✱ 7" x 3" (18 x 8cm) Piece of thin batting

✱ Matching sewing thread

CUTTING

1 Cut the template on page 120.

2 Using the template, cut the diamond from the 2 ½" (6.5cm) squares.

3 Lay out your pieces in the desired pattern.

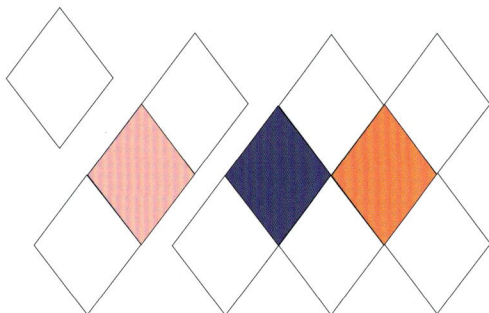

SEWING

4 When sewing the diamonds the pieces need to be off-set slightly so that when the seams open they line up evenly.

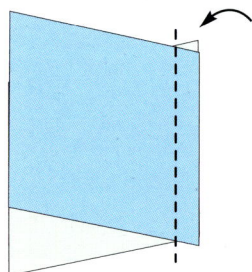

5 Sew the rows together so that the seams are offset again. You may wish to pin them together and test out a row first with large stitches in case you need to remove them. There will be movement in the pieces because they are cut on the bias slightly. Sewing slowly and checking the seams can be helpful.

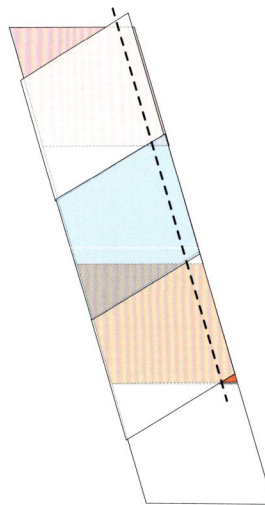

6 Press all seams. Layer with batting and lining and quilt as desired. I quilted it to create an argyle look.

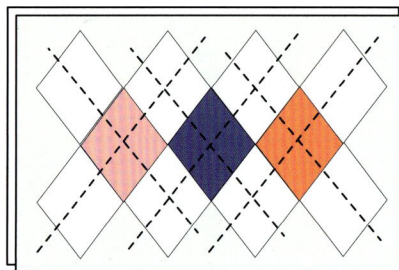

7 Cut the bottom pieces into; 3" x 7" (8 x 18cm), two – 3" x 5 ½" (8 x 14cm). With right sides facing stitch the two 3" x 5 ½" (8 x 14cm) pieces together at the ends.

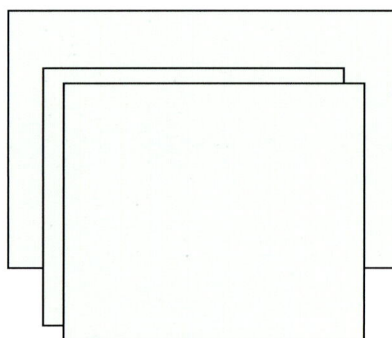

8 Fold the seam over and press. Layer it on top of the 3" x 7" (8 x 18cm) piece.

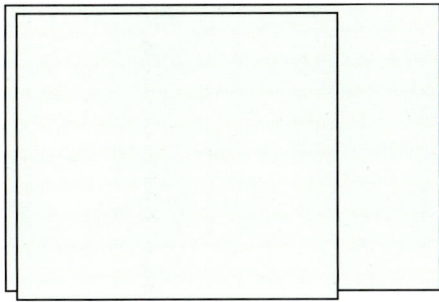

9 Stitch it on either side to hold it in place.

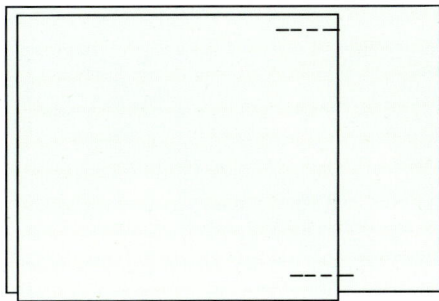

10 Fold the strawberry fabric in half lengthwise and line it up along the long side of a blue 2" x 7" (5 x 18cm) side piece. This is the side pocket piece.

11 Stitch the blue 2" x 3" (5 x 8cm) end peices to either end of the side pocket piece.

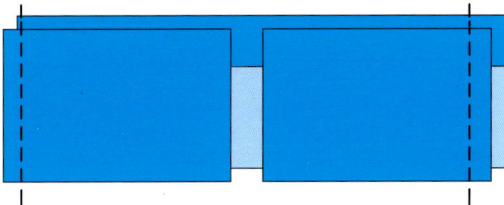

12 Then sew the other 2" x 7" (5 x 18cm) piece to create a loop.

13 Line up the blue side pieces to the pincushion top. Clip the corners to help you as you sew.

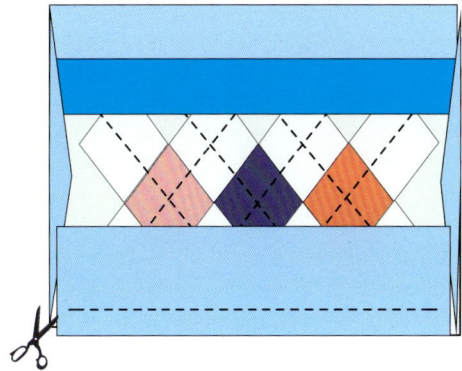

14 Sew it all the way around the pincushion top.

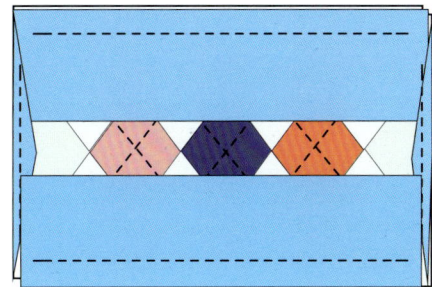

15 Sew the pocket bottom in the same way, beginning at one end. Leave one end open to turn as shown.

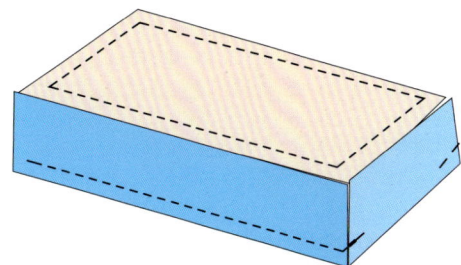

16 Turn right side out and fold the edges in. Hand stitch the opening with tiny stitches.

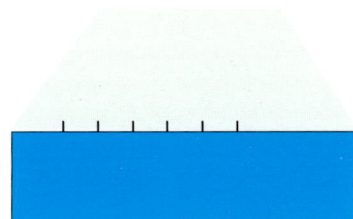

TEMPLATES

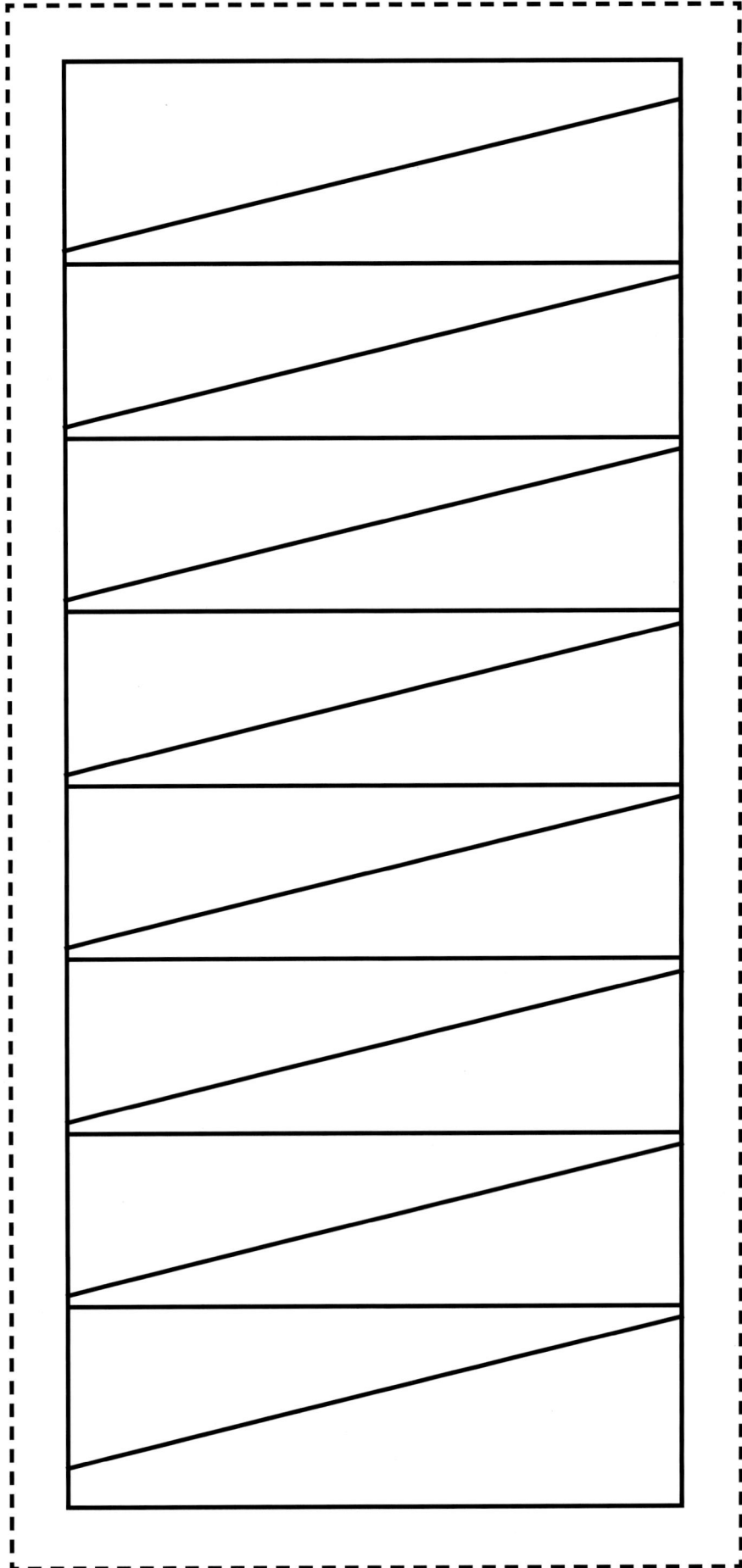

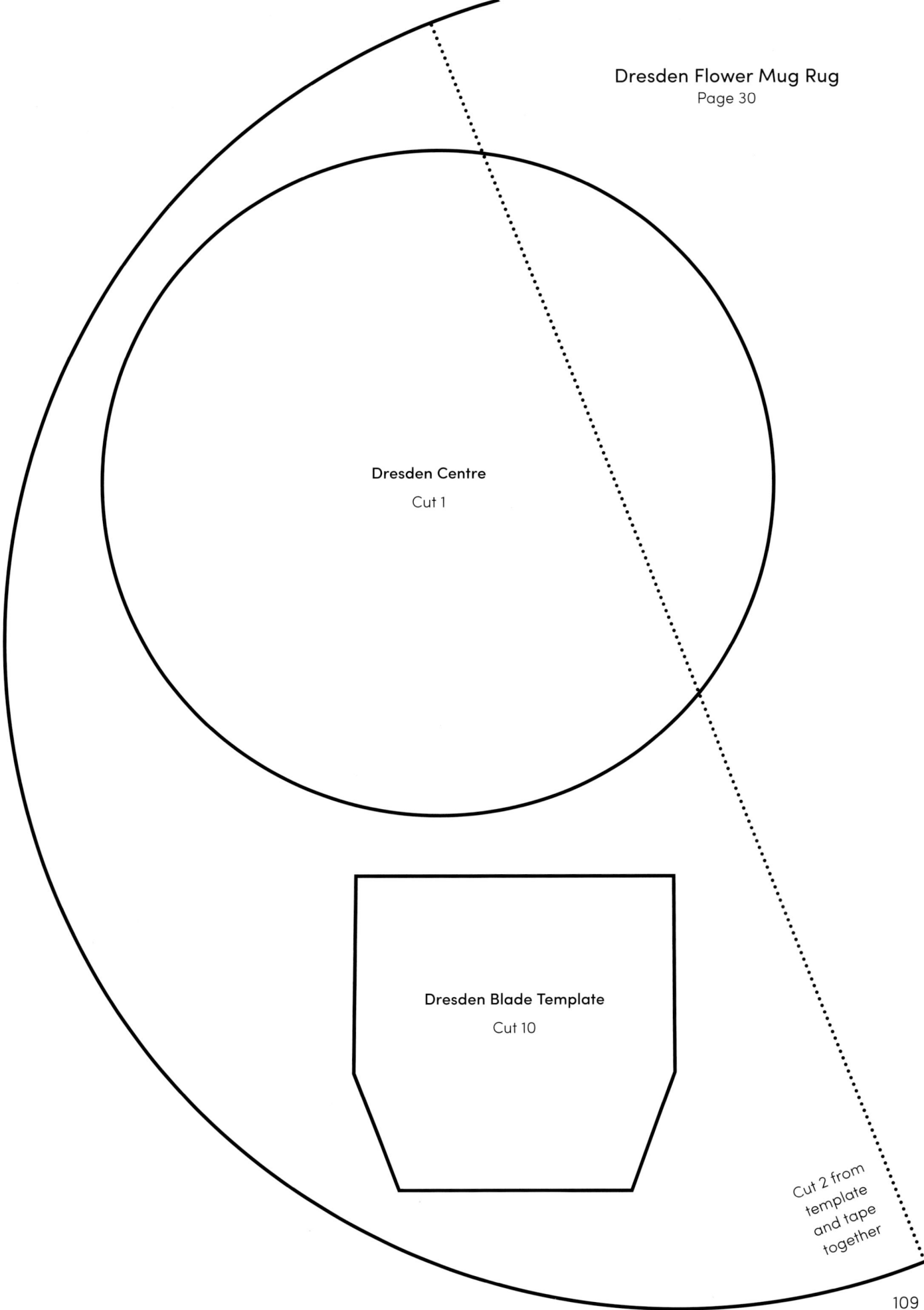

Dresden Centre

Cut 1

Dresden Blade Template

Cut 10

Cut 2 from template and tape together

35 32 29 26 23 20 17 14 11 8 7 2

34 28 22 16 10 4 1 5 13 18 24 30 36

3

6 9

12 15

19 21

25 27

31 33

37

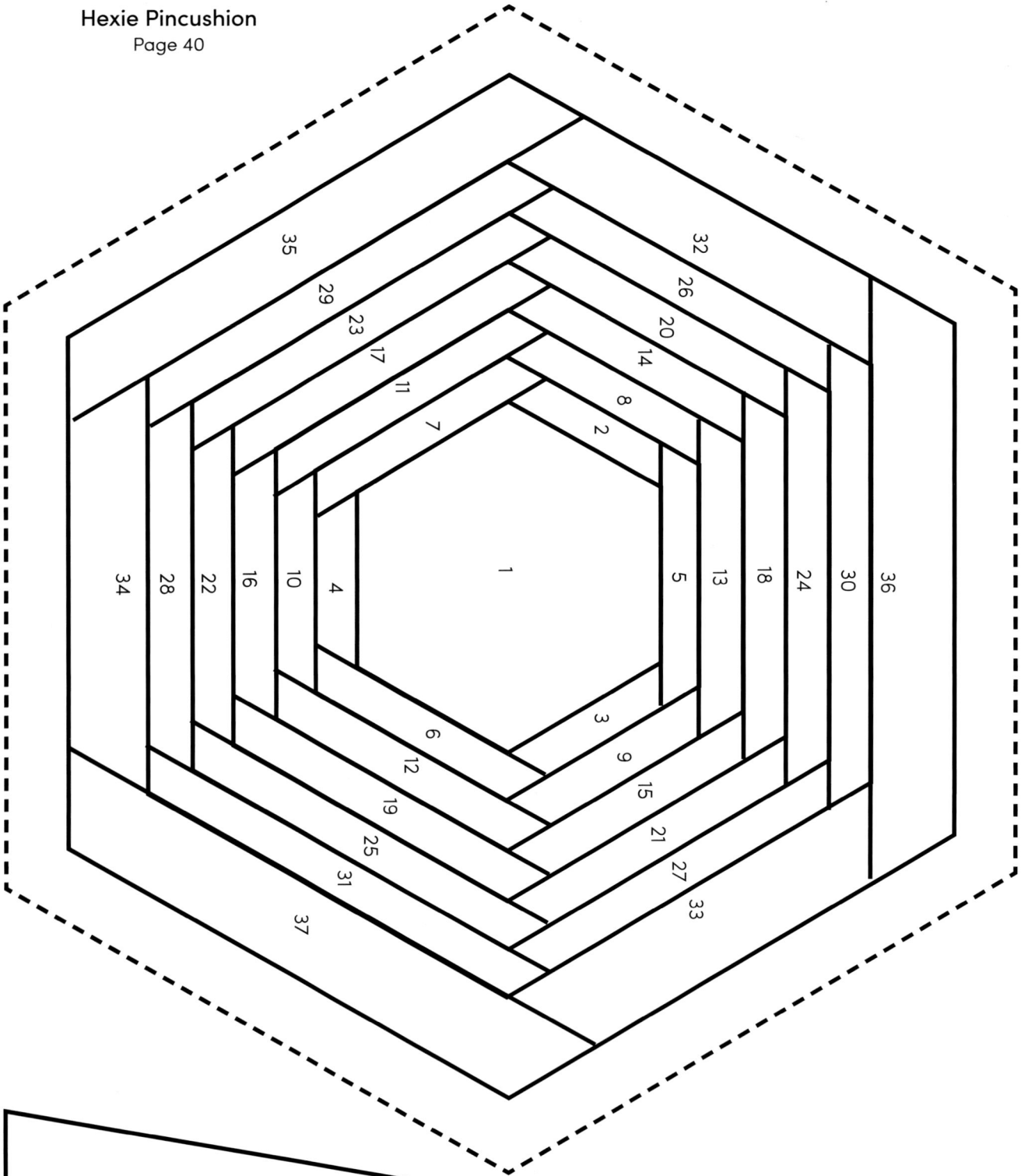

Rainbow Prism Wall Hanging
Page 56

1" (2.5cm)
Template
Size Guide

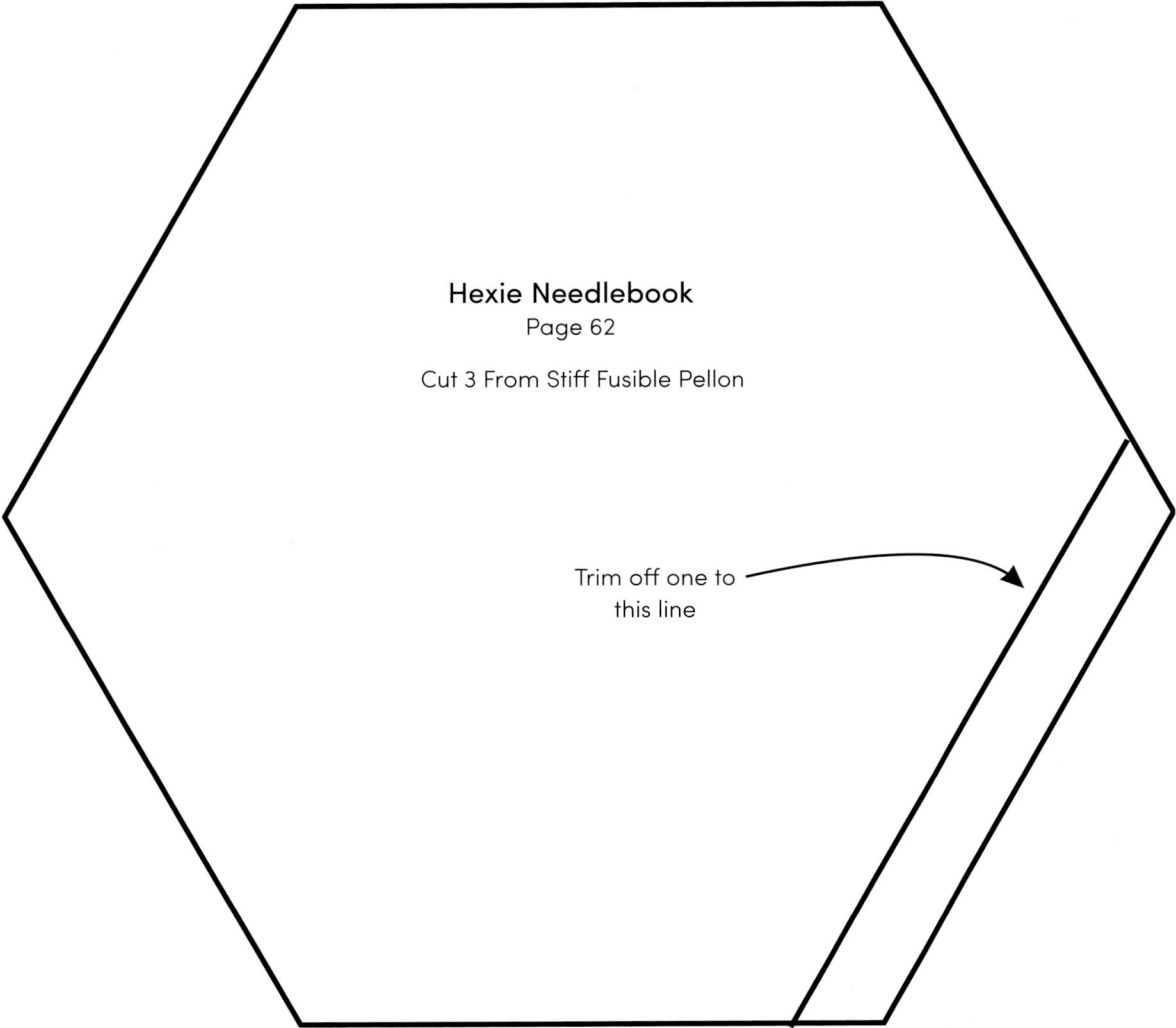

Hexie Needlebook
Page 62

Cut 3 From Stiff Fusible Pellon

Trim off one to
this line

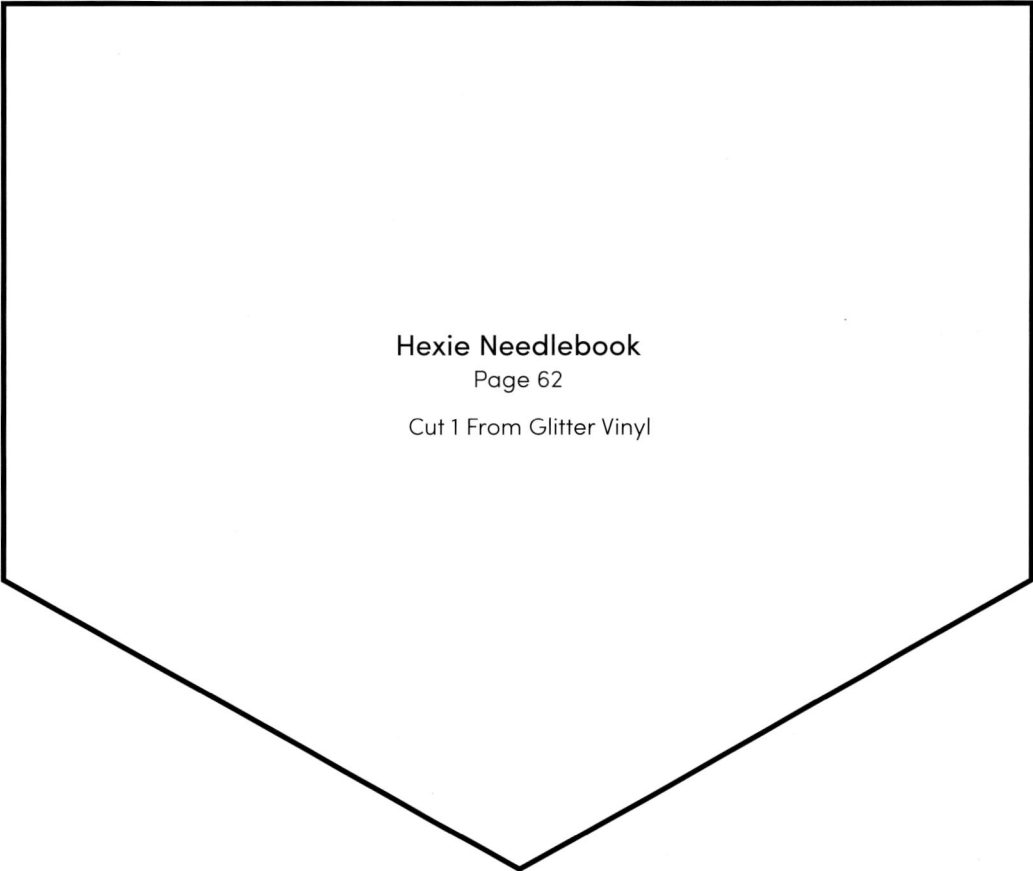

Hexie Needlebook
Page 62

Cut 1 From Glitter Vinyl

Print 2
Match Along Dotted Line

Hexie Needlebook
Page 62

Cut 1 From Pink Fabric

Cut 1 From Thin Batting

Hexie Needlebook
Page 62

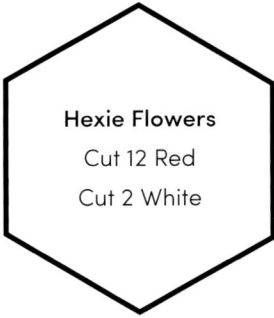

Hexie Flowers

Cut 12 Red

Cut 2 White

Quilt Clip Centre

Cut 2 From White Fabric

Cut 1 From Batting

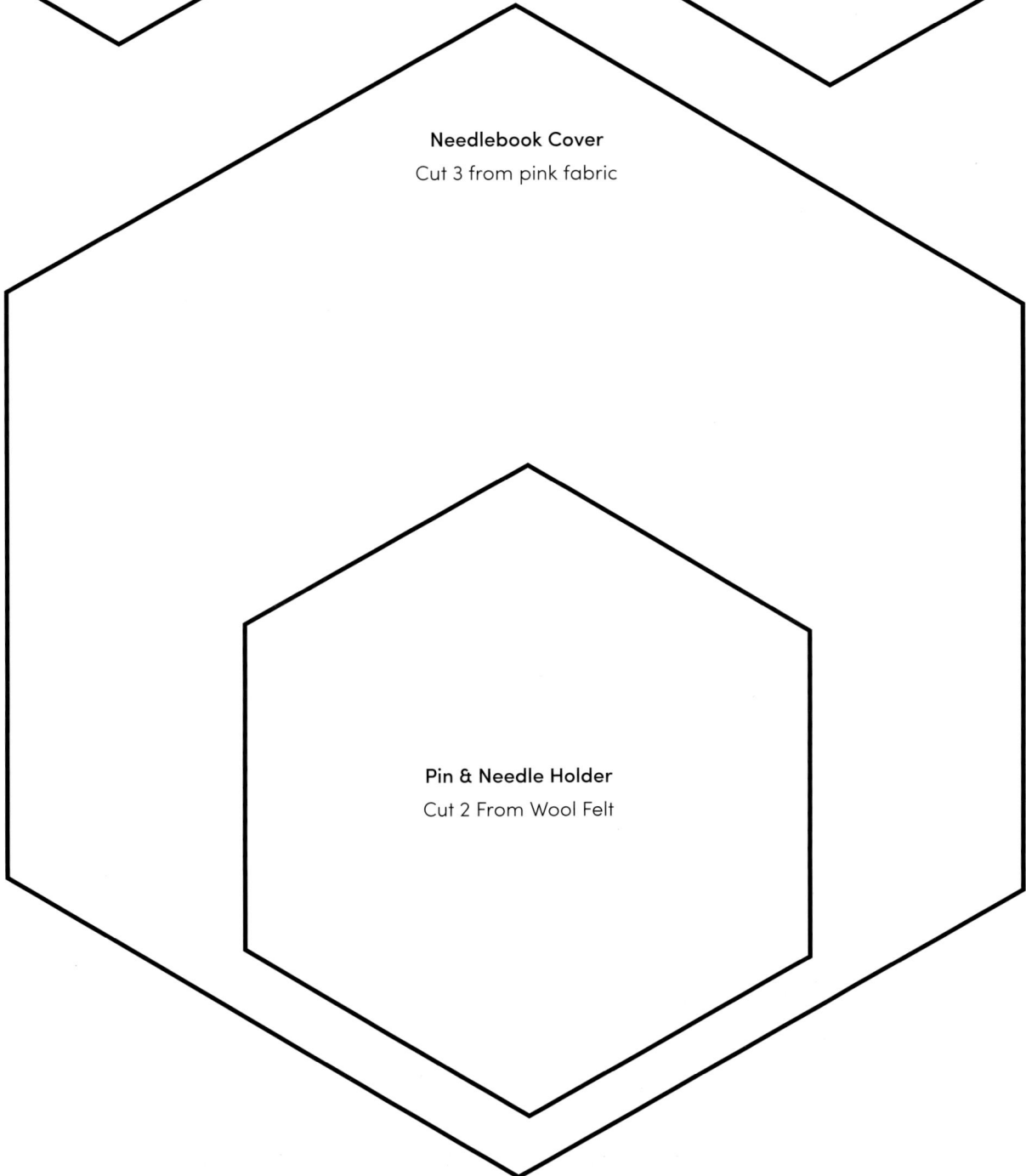

Needlebook Cover

Cut 3 from pink fabric

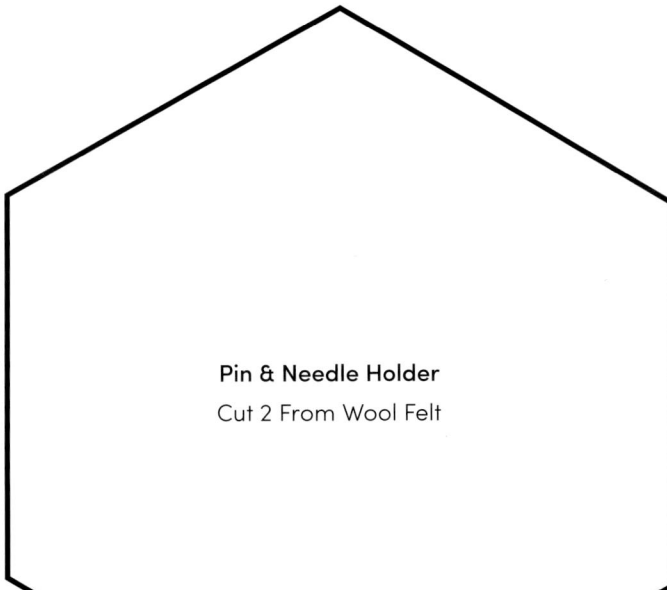

Pin & Needle Holder

Cut 2 From Wool Felt

Berry Busy Pack
Page 72

Cut the templates
and tape together

Berry Busy Pack Bottom

Berry Busy Pack

Cut the templates
and tape together

Cut the templates
and tape together

Berry Busy Pack
Page 72

Berry Busy Pack Bottom

Berry Busy Pack

Cut 20 – 22

Cut the templates
and tape together

Berry Busy Pack
Page 72

Cut the templates
and tape together

Berry Busy Pack Side

Berry Busy Pack Flap

Cut the templates
and tape together

Berry Busy Pack

Template for hexie quilting
if desired

Cut the templates
and tape together

Cut the templates
and tape together

Cut the templates
and tape together

Berry Busy Pack Side

Berry Busy Pack Flap

Cut the templates
and tape together

Berry Busy Pack
Page 72

Cut the templates
and tape together

Cut the templates
and tape together

Fold

Berry Busy Pack Front

1" (2.5cm)
Template
Size Guide

Cut 2 from templates
and tape together

Log Cabin Mini
Page 90

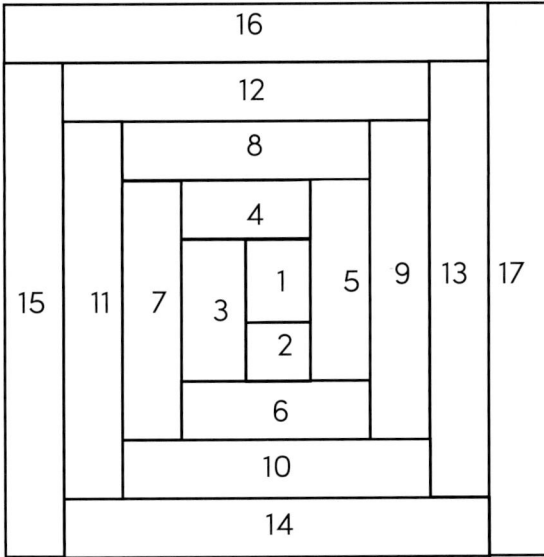

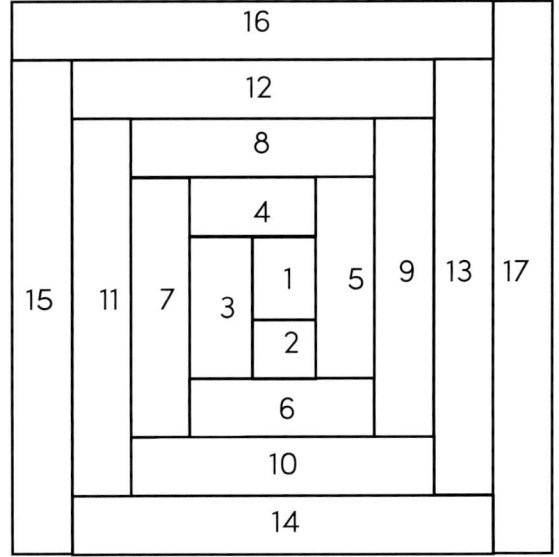

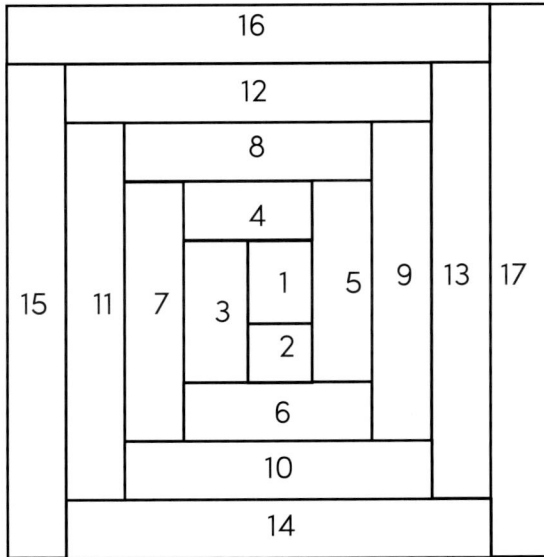

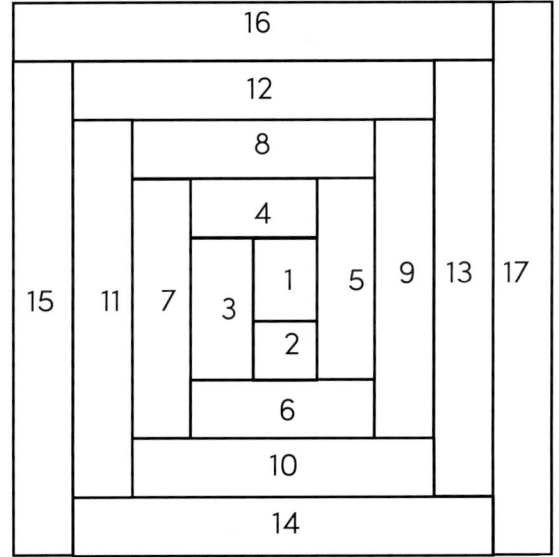

Log Cabin Mini
Page 90

Diamond Pincushion
Page 102

Diamond Template

Pouch Purse
Page 96

Print 4 and tape
together matching
dotted lines.